Visitors at the End of Life

Visitors at the End of Life

Finding Meaning and Purpose in Near-Death Phenomena

ALLAN KELLEHEAR

COLUMBIA UNIVERSITY PRESS
New York

Columbia University Press
Publishers Since 1893
New York   Chichester, West Sussex
cup.columbia.edu
Copyright © 2020 Columbia University Press
All rights reserved

Library of Congress Cataloging-in-Publication Data
Names: Kellehear, Allan, 1955– author.
Title: Visitors at the end of life : finding meaning and purpose in near-death phenomena / Allan Kellehear.
Description: New York : Columbia University Press, [2020] | Includes bibliographical references and index.
Identifiers: LCCN 2019057375 (print) | LCCN 2019057376 (ebook) | ISBN 9780231182140 (hardback) | ISBN 9780231182157 (paperback) | ISBN 9780231544023 (ebook)
Subjects: LCSH: Deathbed hallucinations. | Near-death experiences. | Spirits—Social aspects. | Death—Social aspects.
Classification: LCC BF1063.D4 K45 2020 (print) | LCC BF1063.D4 (ebook) | DDC 133.9—dc23
LC record available at https://lccn.loc.gov/2019057375
LC ebook record available at https://lccn.loc.gov/2019057376

COVER IMAGE: Pym V (dark), 2018
© Stephen Dow/Private Collection/Bridgeman Images

COVER DESIGN:
Chang Jae Lee

> Be ye lamps unto yourselves
> > Be your own reliance
> > > Hold to the truth within yourselves
> > Be the lamp
> > > > —Buddha

Contents

Preface ix

PART I
Conflict and Context

1
Visitors Near Death: Are They "Real"? 3

2
Hallucinations 21

3
Perception 39

PART II
Patterns of Custom and Solicitation

4
Greetings and Other Customs 63

Contents

5
Advice   80

6
Transformation   96

7
Gifts   113

PART III
A Pattern Directing the Patterns

8
Vigils   133

Conclusion   150

Acknowledgments   159

Notes   163

Bibliography   181

Index   193

Preface

FROM 2009 TO 2012, I conducted deathbed studies with medical colleagues in India[1] and in the Republic of Moldova in Eastern Europe.[2] We interviewed the dying and the bereaved on the experiences of those near death. In both studies, the general prevalence of deathbed visions was about 30 percent. In the Moldovan study, family commonly reported that the dying person felt supported or "assisted" in some way by their visions: "He dreamed that his dead mother had come through the door. It happened in the last few days, he spoke often about this and would say that his mother was coming to get him. He would ask if I could see her too, he was saying this with his eyes open, he would say a few times a day that his mother had come."[3] For other dying people, visits from the dead provided them with companionship. Sometimes the visitors were intimates such as parents, and other times they were former friends and villagers. "I don't know if she had 'visions' but she would often be in a trance when she spoke to my father, who was dead, or with my mother (likewise, she had been dead many years), and she would also speak to a child."[4] And again: "Yes, he had visions. He would look out of the window and call people who were already dead to come to him inside the house. He would tell me he could see them looking at him. He saw several dead people. He practically listed all our neighbors and relatives who had long died."[5] The bereavement researchers Bill Guggenheim and Judy Guggenheim describe the story of a woman named Sonia, who spoke to them about her nine-year-old daughter Valerie, who had died suddenly of a brain hemorrhage. On an evening about six weeks after Valerie's death, Sonia recounts:

> I went to bed quite early because I had exhausted myself, but I know I was awake. I was lying on my right side, and I felt someone touch my shoulder. I turned over and Valerie was standing there! She seemed real to me. She looked exactly like herself and in good health. She was bright, sort of glowing, and was dressed in a sparkling, dazzling white gown. She said, "Mommy, I love you. My headache is gone. I'm all right, and I don't want you to worry about me." She was very calm and happy and quite beautiful. Then, suddenly, she was gone.[6]

This book explores our personal experience of visitations by our dead. It is not designed or intended to establish where the dead come from, whether these appearances are some form of hallucination, whether they are pathological, whether they arise from mental illness or organic anomalies. We do not know whether they point reliably to personal survival over death. What we do know is that a large minority of people all over the world commonly experience contact with their dead—sometimes regularly, sometimes as one-offs—and that there is both an academic and a personal need to know why.

We can establish a broad outline of why the dead contact us by reflecting on a range of typical accounts drawn from the many thousands of personal accounts in books, articles, and social media sources. We can supplement these descriptions and reflections with the long-standing anthropological and folkloric writing about the patterns of assumptions and interaction behind the conduct of the visiting dead. Sometimes, these dead are accompanied by friends, such as beings of light. Where this is the case, we also employ the same methods to understand their behavior.

My first aim in this work is to sketch an outline of an approach to visits from our dead that frequently emerge from the main mystical experiences near death—from among near-death experiences, deathbed visions, or visions encountered by bereaved people. I offer insights into why our dead appear to us by drawing inferences and deductions from the usual reasons why the dead tend to visit in other people's societies and drawing on some of the key rituals governing all human interaction, identifying the purpose and meaning underlying those, and then applying these to our visitation events. The anthropological view has long been that these experiences of visitation are best viewed as extensions of normal, everyday social life. For many traditional societies, that is the normal view. For most modern societies with industrial economies, that view is not.

But like it or not, the appearances of the dead in all societies are not in any way deterred by the fact that some are prepared for their appearance and others are not. The dead come anyway—everywhere. Neither cultural receptivity nor antipathy seems to slow down their appearances among us. The only difference is that more traditional societies have a ready set of explanations for what is going on, and the peoples from the industrial economies do not. An anthropological perspective such as the one I offer here can bridge that gap in our own sense and sensibility toward this enigmatic experience.

It does not matter whether these appearances originate from the mind or from a genuine afterlife reality. What matters most is the social impacts and personal consequences on those who encounter these experiences. In my line of work—hospice and palliative care—I meet many people who are affected by these common (and commonly difficult to speak about) experiences. Many of them are made uncomfortable, even distressed, when speaking about these experiences—not because the apparitions upset them (they rarely do!) but because other people's reactions are so fearful, suspicious, undermining, or dismissive.

On the one hand, so many people think these visits are isolated or freak incidents when they are not. On the other hand, other people commonly believe that the only real questions concern the origins of these visits, but these are not, for those who have them, the key concerns. These perspectives miss both the value and the point of these visitations. At best, they trivialize the people attempting to speak about them. At worst, they marginalize them. There has been a serious gap in ways to talk about these visits that normalizes these types of experiences and the conversations that attempt to discuss them. The second aim of this book, then, is to redress that omission.

I will describe, reflect on, and argue that the ultimate source of these visits from the dead is far less important than understanding the reasons they come into people's lives in the first place, and what it is they often ask from each of us when they do. This is a humanistic exercise in establishing the social logic behind both the behavior and the motivations in these visits. Their ultimate source does not alter this particular dimension of the experience. Where the postman comes from is far less important than what is delivered.

In their book *The Social Life of Spirits*,[7] the anthropologists Ruy Blanes and Diana Espírito Santo argue that it is not only "spirits" who are "invisible" but much of the world we call "culture." We cannot see the so-called market or so-called race. These ideas are not personally tried and tested; they are subjects of social debate and theorizing. There is even debate about the origin of these ideas. All that most of us know is that these ideas are central to our life, and we must make personal sense of them to negotiate our way through, alongside, against, or above and beyond them. Blanes and Santos argue, as I do, that the key question most people ask when they have these experiences is not whether dead beings exist or where they come from but why they have come and how that contact has changed our lives. In the matter of understanding "spirits," the purpose of an anthropological perspective is to go beyond psychology, neuroscience, or the metaphysical and understand the social meaning. This is the fundamental task before us.

I spend the first few chapters of the book making the argument that we need to take a different, more social approach to appearances of our dead. I then examine how the natural biases in our everyday perceptual machinery predispose us to see the unusual anyway, and how this might aid the perception of the unusual, both near-death and inside experiences of loss. The remaining chapters characterize the key patterns of behavior that the dead and their being-of-light friends seem to demonstrate—customs of greeting, advice and solicitation, transformative or reorienting influences, and the politics of gift exchange. In the final chapter, I show how each of these characteristic pieces of conduct falls into a broad class of conduct known as "keeping vigil"—the dead seem to watch over us, a type of conduct we displayed toward them when they were alive but ill or dying. It seems, then, like so much else in life, their conduct here is a mirror of our own.

I have written this book for the general reader. It is a collection not simply of academic argument and references but also of case study and personal reflection. Where I think the arguments could benefit from a tighter line of support I have referenced heavily. Where I find myself on less controversial ground, I have referenced more lightly. I have written this book mainly to encourage a more thoughtful approach to a reoccurring enigma at the center of our personal and social experiences.

PART I
Conflict and Context

1

Visitors Near Death

Are They "Real"?

IN 1926, THE PHYSICS PROFESSOR William Barrett described a remarkable incident associated with a dying school-aged child. The account is retold by the dying child's brother, who was present at the time:

> She knew she was passing away, and was telling her mother how to dispose of her little personal belongings among her close friends and playmates, when she suddenly raised her eyes as though gazing at the ceiling toward the farther side of the room, and after looking steadily and apparently listening for a short time, slightly bowed her head, and said, "Yes, Grandma, I am coming, only just wait a little while, please." Our father asked her, "Hattie, do you see your grandma?" Seemingly surprised at the question, she promptly answered, "Yes, Papa, can't you see her? She is right there waiting for me." At the same time, she pointed to the ceiling in the direction in which she had been gazing. Again, addressing the vision she evidently had of her grandmother, she scowled a little impatiently and said, "Yes, Grandma, I'm coming,

but wait a minute, please." She then turned once more to her mother and finished telling her what of her personal treasures to give to different ones of her acquaintances. At last, giving her attention once more to her Grandma, who was apparently urging her to come at once, she bade each of us good-bye. Her voice was very feeble and faint, but the look in her eyes as she glanced briefly at each of us was as lifelike and as intelligent as it could be. She then fixed her eyes steadily on her vision but so faintly that we could just catch her words, said, "Yes, Grandma, I'm coming now." Then without a struggle or evidence of pain of any kind she gazed steadily in the direction she had pointed out to us where she saw her Grandma, until the absence of oxygen in her bloodstream, because respiration had ceased, left her hands and face all covered with the pallor of lifeless flesh.[1]

In 2009 I was part of a large medical study examining the last days and hours of life for palliative care patients in India.[2] We interviewed one hundred families about their loved ones' last days. In one of these interviews, I came upon a remarkable story of another child whose experience seemed to parallel the one I have recounted above:

Anita was an eight-year-old girl dying of AIDS but with no medical history of opioid or painkiller use. In the week leading up to her death, her prescribed pharmacotherapy consisted of some anti-emetics, antibiotics, and antivirals, but most of these were refused by the child during this period. On the day that she died, Anita announced to her mother, in a very matter of fact way, that her late grandmother had come to sit with her. Her grandmother had died four months previously. The grandmother would sit beside her and chat, occasionally calling for her. "*Amma*" ("Mother" in the local language) she had said, "don't hug or hold me anymore; don't put me on your lap because it's time for me to go, so don't do any of these things for me. I need to go now." And later that day she died.[3]

I often recount these two stories side by side because of their remarkable similarities. I tell these stories in the classroom and sometimes at dinner with friends where I am often prevailed on to speak about some of my fieldwork with dying people around the world. And the common reactions I get to their retelling reflect the widespread reactions of popular literature and news stories about these accounts. How fascinating and exciting, some will remark. Does this make you believe in an afterlife? (No, it does not.) These events must be very affirming of the viewpoint that we all survive death, or at the very least, suggest that there is good evidence that we do. (No, they are not.) Others will nod sadly or sagely (this especially depends on the public self one is trying to sell at dinner parties). These stories, the wise heads will declare, are clear evidence of hallucinations near death that we so often hear about. (No, they are not.)

My stories of children's deathbed visions will then stimulate remembered stories from the popular press or internet videos about near-death experiences and how these are the result of oxygen starvation of the brain as it dies. Neuroscientific research has repeatedly shown that as the dying person slips toward death the brain's oxygen levels deplete until, near starvation, the brain's neurons begin to misfire and the person is bombarded by random memories, bright lights, and out-of-body experiences.[4] Disordered thinking and feeling occur near death. If not dementia, then it seems delirium awaits us all at death's door.

These divided but ardently held views illustrate that people never seem to tire of two things: being certain about uncertain things and taking an adversarial binary approach to any problem. It never ceases to surprise me how few audiences respond to these stories with contemplative silence. Instead—repeatedly—my listeners reach for the two great preformed conclusions on this topic. Most people in the world today believe in a life beyond death. Many Americans also believe that human beings survive death to go on to "another world." Many of these believers do not need to read books about deathbed visions, near-death experiences, or visions of the bereaved to affirm their a priori beliefs.[5] This is especially true of those with, or influenced by, so-called New Age persuasions: those who love astrology, Eastern religions, Western Spiritualism, or pagan traditions of mysticism.

On the other hand, there are those who believe that neuroscience has won the day and that anything that cannot be explained through the latest research on genetics or hallucinations (or speculative extensions thereupon) is just a new theory of the boogeyman. "Normal" and "reasonable" people look for the rational explanation.

There is just one problem with these two divided approaches. Neither of them is true.

Religions have little or no evidence for what their own theological theorists describe as *eschatology*, the final picture of where souls eventually go after death: heaven, hell, reincarnation. There is no so-called evidence of life after death. There are some good arguments,[6] some of them based on empirical facts that one might interpret as strongly indicative. That is certainly true. And the research into hallucinations is woefully underdeveloped and surprisingly, even shockingly speculative. There has not even been general agreement on what the definition of a hallucination actually is in the past two hundred years of academic research into this topic. There are some good arguments, some of them based on good animal and clinical experiments that one might interpret as strongly indicative of cerebral anomalies.

But let me say clearly at the outset of this book that, on the matter of unusual visitors near death, popular confidence in both religion and science is misplaced. I will return to this observation very soon, but for now we are left with the one important question: If telling stories of greetings and solicitations near death or personally encountering these kinds of visions and visitors is not bulk fodder either for the great debates on human survival after death or for the idea that the brain works as an electric motor for consciousness, well then, what is left? What other question, if any, is worth pursuing?

WHEN CONSIDERING what questions remain to ask, if we cannot ask the fashionable but empty ones, let us remind ourselves of the social context of intellectual inquiry—how sometimes seeking an answer to one particular social question (e.g., Where did Joe go?) can marginalize more important questions about one's immediate and prospective social experience (e.g., How will Joe's absence affect us?). Dying and grieving are *social* experiences—they are not essentially religious or neurological experiences, even though they have those dimensions.

I was on a train one winter day in Hokkaido, Japan. We were traveling back from Wakkanai in the far north of that island to the capital, Sapporo, in the south. There was snow everywhere—on the passing farms, woods, and hillsides. About a third of the way into our trip, the train came to a sudden stop. We remained stopped for about thirty minutes—nowhere near a railway siding or station, but in the middle of a forest glade sliced through by the path of the rail tracks. A conductor walked back and forth during that time, maybe twice, maybe three times.

People started to talk and speculate. The train had broken down. The train had been stopped by a large snowdrift across the lines, or perhaps a fallen pine tree. Yes, that was it. The train either had broken down or had been stopped by a winter accident. The passengers in the carriage I was in entertained themselves with this debate.

Some spoke speculatively. Others "knew." Those who "knew" supported their side of the explanation with authority: they had been traveling on this very train during this time of the year "many, many" times before. Experience gave them the appearance of wisdom. Many found this charismatic, even irresistibly attractive. Others were irritated by this commuter arrogance and forged on to advocate the "alternative" view of our predicament. The conductor was clearly worried, they argued. The conductor could be heard, though somewhat inaudibly, communicating back and forth with the driver of the train. It was a mechanical problem. One daring passenger provided some empirical basis for this argument. He managed to peer outside the train through a faulty window and could see no snowdrift or fallen tree, though even he had to admit he could not see directly in front of the lead carriage. It was a friendly debate by a collection of strangers who passed the time as though they were playing a game. It was a social scene more at home in the scribbles of Bill Bryson than those of Franz Kafka.

Finally, the conductor made an announcement over the train loudspeakers. Great apologies to all passengers for the inconvenience and for delayed communication. The train was stopped because there was a deer lying on the track, and quite a few yards away from that deer was a bear, also dawdling about on the track. Usually, if a deer is found on the track, a few blows on the train horn and the deer will move on. If this is insufficient, the driver will usually dismount from his carriage and shoo it off the track. But on this occasion, he dared not leave the carriage because of the bear. After half an hour the bear and the deer apparently moved on of their own accord, and our train continued on.

The passengers' debate had failed to arrive at any conclusions remotely resembling the final explanation. The knowing heads were too invested in "knowing," and the alternative explainers were too invested in challenging them. None of them at that time knew the full spectrum of what is possible for trains to encounter in rural Hokkaido in the dead of winter. The two possibilities offered were not up to the job. Is there more to know in these circumstances than merely the science of causal explanation? For example, why not ask what happened during those thirty minutes?

Here is what happened. (1) The train was delayed. (2) People who had been strangers before got to know one another—commuters, tourists, foreigners, locals, men and women, young people and old. (3) Most had fun. (4) Passengers bought more from the mobile catering service inside the train. (5) The journey would be known for the quality of the social experience notwithstanding the unserviceable conclusions drawn for why the train had been delayed. (6) The *accuracy* of the final explanation had no impact on the social outcomes of the day—being late, having fun, eating more, meeting others. When all is said and done, it is the quality of the social experience that is important to people, rather than any intellectual or academic satisfaction about their own personal theories of train delay.

It is the same in other endeavors. In medicine or in laboratory science or in agriculture, it is unwise to invest too quickly in two possible hypotheses. When a problem presents, no matter how many times it has presented before, we are unwise to assume that the same causal processes are operating. A pain in the chest may indicate heart disease or respiratory distress, but it could just as easily be a gastric ulcer or gallstone obstruction or psychosomatic anxiety. The final explanation will be important, but it is not *absolutely and supremely* important. The first and most important priority is the patient's comfort and safety. A diagnosis is important, but so is symptom control. Diagnosis is difficult if the patient is screaming and writhing on a hospital gurney. The science of healing and the art of healing are different, but they complement each other.

What is the quality of the social experience of being visited by the dead or beings of light? Is it scary? Is it comforting? How do we know? What happens when we suddenly see such visitors? Do they follow any rules or customs? Are they unpredictable and occult, or can we know why they come? For what purpose do they visit? Is there a pattern of meaning that we can discern? What models of human behavior can we use to extrapolate and extend to these beings and their visits, particularly if we move away from supernatural or neurological explanations?

In the end, what do these strange visits mean to the person who experiences them?

This is a book about the meaning that can be made from the greetings and solicitations people encounter when they are near death. To do this, I use traditional insights drawn from anthropology, sociology, and communication science. Our purpose in this book, then, is to move away from "final" explanations, which I believe are far too narrow and adversarial to be of much use and rather academic when faced with death or loss in real time. Instead, we will focus on what is far more important for us when we die and grieve. The real questions are: What are these beings that are so commonly reported in circumstances of death, dying, and bereavement? Why do they visit us, and how do they change the experience of dying and grieving?

Let us begin with the question of who these visitors are.

The Inexplicable Calls

Most unexpected visitors come to us from three main corridors of experience. These are near-death experiences (NDEs), deathbed visions (DBVs), and visions of the bereaved (VBs).

NDEs are commonly associated with medical emergencies such as a heart attack. After being resuscitated, recovered people may report a series of unusual events, which they believe occurred to them when everyone else presumed them to be fully unconscious or even dead. These include a sensation of being out-of-body, often viewing the medical team during their attempts to resuscitate the patient. Sometimes recovered people report a tunnel sensation. Many detail other experiences beyond these: they might report meeting a bright "being of light." The being of light frequently helps them review their life. Sometimes people then meet previously deceased friends and relatives in a beautiful supernatural environment.

The being of light is an unusual encounter because it is not prima facie a human encounter, although we cannot rule this out entirely. We simply do not know. But if you were to predict that you would see beings in the afterlife or in your hallucinations as you were near death, you would probably predict that you would see your dead relatives rather than a being that has no precedent in your day-to-day life. That said, there is always someone who will find a possibility even here. For example, some may argue that beings of light are described well enough in the Bible or other holy books. Perhaps that is why this detail may creep into the unconscious experiences of those near death. But it is not a persuasive hypothesis, mainly because there are many others who have had an NDE and who are unfamiliar with such texts. The being of light remains an enigma.

The journalist Ian Wilson describes the NDE of a man that begins, like so many others, with an out-of-body experience. The man finds himself flying over the rooftops of Bristol, England, then traveling down a tunnel before appearing in a supernatural environment where he meets the dead—including his recently deceased father.[7] Not long after this he describes a new and even more fantastic encounter: "I came into the presence of the 'Being of Light.'" By the experiencer's own admission, this was "absolutely incredible . . . a total peace, an indescribable total peace. . . . It was like being inside a soft gold neon tube, you were enveloped in this . . . one I don't hesitate to call God."[8]

The Australian journalist Bruce Elder describes the example of a fourteen-year-old named Allan, who, while drowned, recalls meeting several deceased relatives and a being of light.[9] In this case, the being of light is introduced by several of his deceased friends who warned the percipient that the being was coming. "It was quite white," Allan recalls, "an ivory tape of light. It came rushing forward at an immense speed. It was a very big light and it was the brightest light I've ever seen in all my life but it didn't hurt my eyes. . . . The peace increased as the light got closer and when the light was there I don't think I ever felt better in all my life."[10] The being of light then commences to ask Allan about the life he is leading.

The doctor Melvin Morse, in his review of children's NDEs, observed that those who experience the light report that it is more than simply a light experience—it has a substance or effect of wrapping itself around and inside you, conveying great warmth and care.[11] Morse's cases of children's NDEs describe the being of light as one that offers "unconditional love" or that has a demeanor that is "all knowing" or "all forgiving" or "all loving." One respondent described it as "misty" and cloudlike, from inside of which she heard a voice.[12]

But the single presence of a being of light visiting you when you are near death is not without complexity. There seem to be more senior beings of light. The philosopher and doctor Raymond Moody describes it this way:

> After meeting several beings of light, the NDEr usually meets a supreme Being of Light. People with a Christian background often describe him as God or Jesus. Those with other religious backgrounds may call him Buddha or Allah. But some have said that it's neither God nor Jesus, but someone very holy nonetheless. Whoever it is, the Being radiates total love and understanding.[13]

You can read hundreds of accounts of these beings of light in any popular or academic book on NDEs, and, of course, you can hear first-person accounts on the internet. From a review of these accounts we can fairly deduce a couple of important conclusions: first, the beings of light may not be what we are traditionally accustomed to expect in another human's shape and appearance; and second, although many, but not all, will describe these as "gods," most of this type of conclusion is an ascription by the observers and not regularly confessed by the beings themselves. It is rare indeed for a being of light to greet someone with, "Hi there. I'm Jesus Christ. So glad you could make it today," or "Welcome, Richard. I'm the Buddha. Take a seat while I look at your file." Like life itself, there seems to be a whole lot of assumptions by the person near death at the initial—and, it must be said—*brief* meeting. And it appears that you do not have to be unconscious and on the actual brink of death to meet a being of light.

The writer Katherine Russell Rich, diagnosed with breast cancer when she was only thirty-two, described a moment of despair that was interrupted by the presence of an unusual light:

> In November a curious thing happened. On the night before my thirty-third birthday, I was lying in bed, face to the wall, crying. Despondence had burned off the Scotch I'd drunk, was propelling me into hysteria. Between sobs, I'd go rigid, and it was in one of those moments of silence that I sensed a presence in the room behind me. Startled, I turned my head and saw a diffuse violet light shining through the bedroom door. The light didn't scare me, it soothed me, in fact, and within seconds, I was calm. Puzzled by this sudden well-being—the tears weren't even dry—I tried to work myself back into hysteria, but couldn't. My anguish had vanished, drained by the light. A sense of security overtook me, the first I felt in years, and soon I was asleep.... Ten years on, the memory remains indelible, still potent and still inexplicable.[14]

So in all these cases, we have what many anthropologists and archaeologists would describe as a "transitional hominid"–style being. What, you might ask, is a transitional hominid being? Transitional hominids are beings that have some human characteristics and some characteristics of another very different species.[15] A good example is the Australopithecus, one of several early species of hominid that had some genetic and morphological characteristics of human beings but also major characteristics of simple, outright primates. They are an intermediary species.

For the beings of light that have been described, we can see typical human characteristics—humor, love, complex and abstract thought, advanced communication and social skills. We may also observe untypical or even nonhuman characteristics: they have been known to fly, they can prompt a life review for those in their charge, many seem androgynous and extremely tall (some eight to twelve feet tall),[16] and of course, they appear to be made of light. They have physical and social characteristics like us, but also other characteristics very *un*like us. They appear to be an intermediary being.

The other major visitors near death, perhaps the largest group of visitors, are our dead. They can be divided up into the recently dead and the long dead. The recently dead are the most likely to visit us during our bereavement period. Although grief is forever, the most intense period—the period when we are most upset and unsettled, when we have insomnia or depression, or when we suffer from an assortment of medical problems such as arrhythmias or gastrointestinal upsets—is the first one or two years. Not long after someone we love has died, the person for whom we grieve may appear to us. One in three people report evidence of this. Some report hearing the voice of the recently dead. Or they may report the strange and unexpected sense of a "presence" in the house where they live. Others may report a full-blown appearance of the recently dead. Commonly the dead do not appear as "ghostly" figures but as reasonably solid-looking figures. There will be eye contact between the recently dead and the bereaved, sometimes even conversational exchanges.

When I was twelve, my piano teacher recounted to me just such an event. She was a middle-aged Dutch immigrant who lived with her mother. She had never married. Piano lessons were offered from her house, and it was not uncommon to see the mother coming and going among the rooms when you were seated at the piano. The mother was in her eighties. One day her mother took a serious turn. I was not sure what it was at the time. It might have been a stroke or a heart problem. But she died some days after being admitted to the hospital from what was clearly a short but fatal illness. Piano lessons were canceled for several weeks.

When I finally returned to lessons, my teacher and I spoke a bit informally about it. I asked where she thought her mother went after death, if anywhere. She replied that she was an atheist and had no belief or hope in any afterlife. The afterlife, she declared, was a story that served children and the religious. I think I felt a bit patronized by that comment, not because I was religious but because I was twelve. Anyway, a couple of months later she kept me awhile after lessons again to tell me about a strange and disturbing occurrence in the house.

My teacher was alone in the house on the day it happened. She went momentarily into her kitchen to collect an orange and a plate and knife, and returned to her sitting room to eat it. Just as she entered the sitting room she saw her dead mother sitting on the sofa. She looked "extremely" well and healthy, even youthful. The dead mother smiled at her daughter, and before my teacher could say anything the deceased disappeared into thin air. The other observation my teacher made was that her mother was wearing the dress she was buried in—a favorite dress, according to my teacher. She recounted this story without emotion. Her affect was flat, as they say in the psychiatry fraternity. On the other hand, I was astonished. How could you not think that was fantastic!

But my teacher was more reserved and thoughtful. She just could not explain it. To her this made no sense, and yet it was her senses she could not question. Of course, she missed her mother, she said. Of course, she was glad her mother looked so well. And then, she confessed a pre-death pact she had made with her mother, who had been a believer in the afterlife. She and her mother were very close. They made a pact—as a remarkable number of people do—that if one of them should die before the other, the dead one would return to offer up evidence of their survival. Her mother, it appeared, had honored the pact.

I asked her if she now believed in an afterlife. She said she could not say. What she would say is that she would now tell anyone who asked her that she was uncertain. Not just about human survival after death, but about God. Although the account was remarkable for its detail and clarity and for the astonishing nature of its content, the most remarkable thing of all was how it seemed to affect my teacher. She clearly took some comfort in the visit, however unexpected, and it had clearly influenced her own views about death and her own experience of grief. It made a difference to her remaining life. The greeting from her mother was life-altering.

The other common type of visitation, a DBV, is from the long dead. The long dead most commonly visit during the dying process. Up to 30 percent of the dying report visits from the dead some days or hours before death.[17] Commonly these figures are parents, and among parents, most often dead mothers. Not absolutely all visitors are long dead, as we saw in the opening case of Anita. Nevertheless, it is more usual that visits come from people who have died years earlier, and that is certainly common in the case of predeceased parents or siblings.

Some years ago, I was in the Republic of Moldova with a team of UNESCO researchers conducting a study of end-of-life care experiences of families looking after their dying loved ones.[18] We interviewed one hundred families about the last days and hours of their care for their dying relative. About one-third of those families reported the occurrence of DBVs of people long dead. One woman reported:

> I noticed something strange one day. We were sitting together in the room, chatting, and at one point mother reproached me that a man from our village—she said who he was and his name, I knew he had died a long time before; he had been friendly with our family and used to sing in the church choir—[she said he] had come wearing a hat and a short-sleeved shirt and was stand-

ing at the door but could not get in because of me. I replied to mother that I did not see anybody around and then she asked me to go outside. I did not leave but continued to stay with her. And then again she said that her mother had this time come to her (I never knew her, she had died before I was born), who, likewise, had been long dead. I again told her I could not see anybody around and mother replied that I could not see them but they had come to get her. And she asked me to leave the door wide open.[19]

In all these cases we see a common set of visitors that seem to have a rather logical pattern of visitation. First, the dead seem to quickly come to the side of the living dying and the bereaved. For the bereaved, this is commonly and not unexpectedly the recently dead. For those on their deathbed, the recently dead may appear too, but because of the epidemiology of modern dying (most people who die are old), most of the visitors are the long dead. Finally, during NDEs both the recent and the long dead may visit during one's brief incursion into the land of the dead. But here we see, often for the first time, a new type of visitor, the being of light.

When we review these kinds of visits from the New Age literature, they are part of a broader narrative about the afterlife. When we review these visitors from the skeptic tradition or dedicated neuroscience literature, we place them in the context of the common symbols, images, and patterns of hallucination and link them to similar patterns in pathological syndromes and diseases like dementia, epilepsy, Charles Bonnet Syndrome, and schizophrenia.

When we make either one of these academic moves, we marginalize or extinguish the question of what customs and conventions the visitors follow and for what exact purpose, as if somehow these do not matter. But the behavior of these visitors, their purpose, and their communications matter very much to those at the center of these experiences. In fact, they are the central questions of all people who have these experiences, and therefore they are, or will be, the central questions for all of us who might experience them in the future.

WHEN WE SEE PEOPLE we love again, but this time around our deathbed, there is the not-insignificant fact that they are actually dead. What are we to make of such events? What can this mean? In my experience, most people are taken up in the immediacy of the moment or moments of the encounter. They are relieved at the temporary reunion, happy to receive a message, reassured of their loved one's safety or well-being, and comforted by their companionship, even if they cannot see them clearly and only have a sense of presence. Even for those who, because of an NDE, will be greeted by a being of light, the encounter is nearly always satisfying, uplifting, and uniquely and positively memorable. This is usually described by those near death as a special moment in their lives, one never to be forgotten.

For those being visited by their dead at their own deathbed, our current research evidence suggests that such visitations are not distressing but comforting. Any cognitive dissonance associated with the fact that they are talking to relatives or friends that are actually dead seems to slip easily away without explanation. It may well be that some people who experience these deathbed visitors do in fact feel awkward or embarrassed by what even they might think initially is irrational or unbelievable. We may never know what proportion make up this group, because they attempt to pass as "normal" so as not to distress or upset their visitors.

However, after most of these encounters, with the possible exception of those who will die in a couple of days or hours after their DBV, most will manage to gain some conscious distance. How, then, do they later make sense of these visits?

They will ask themselves, What does this mean? And commonly when people ask this question, they will eventually ask it jointly with others who might help them with the answer. And this usually means their answers are helped along by those who have not had these experiences.

The literature on the aftermath or the aftereffects of the NDE suggests that when most people share their NDE with family or friends, or worse, a professional person such as a chaplain or counselor, the reactions are not inspiring. Many people, if they do not reel back in horror, will suggest the individuals were hallucinating or suffering some mental aberration related to their illness. Some NDErs have encountered fearful responses from fundamentalist Christians who assumed the beings of light and the visions of the dead were satanic tricks.

Sometimes, if a person who has been visited by the dead has a conservative or anxious background, the person may feel as though he or she is going mad. It is not uncommon for such individuals to self-diagnose or question their own mental stability.

In a secular society where there are few or no traditional frameworks for us to understand visions of the dead or supernatural beings, the largest pool of explanatory resources is psychiatry, psychology, neurology, psychoanalysis—or religion. And most religions do not provide frameworks for understanding these kinds of visitations. Although the Bible does record visits by the dead, including Jesus himself, and by angels, the explanatory narratives are commonly religious rather than social in nature. The visitors in the Bible have not arrived to offer companionship, reassurance, or social comfort.

This means that so often the attempt to ask what it means will lead us back to unhelpful hallucination theory or pop social psychology about cultural reproduction. We see what we expect to see. Either we will lead ourselves into the cultural impasse of the science-or-religion binary, or we will be led by others with the best of intentions into this dead end. It seems that we will not get far in this book without first wrestling with this problem. Let us, then, address these questions so that we can clear the way to answer the new and more important question about this old experience.

Although theories of hallucination are new and evolving and progressing all the time, their current limitations make them unhelpful here. Furthermore, the most interesting and thoughtful research about hallucinations is interdisciplinary. It strikes a balance between, on the one hand, understanding the pathology of hearing voices and seeing things others do not and, on the other, the well-being aspects of these experiences. In other words—and this is crucial to know at the outset of this book—seeing things that others do not see or hear is not only common but also not necessarily a sign of pathology. Those who see and hear things that "are not there" are the majority of people. This is the elephant in the room of psychology and psychiatry.

2

Hallucinations

I WAS AT LUNCH one day with two colleagues from psychiatry, and the conversation veered onto the topic of near-death experiences (NDEs). At that time I had been interviewing patients with life-limiting illnesses for a study, and some of these people were patients under the care of my lunch companions.

One of those patients described her NDE to me, and I relayed this experience at lunch. I had just finished detailing how, while undergoing surgery, this patient had recounted being visited by her dead father during an out-of-body experience. A knowing smile came over one of their faces as we considered this account. I asked what my friends from psychiatry thought had actually happened to this woman.

The woman was hallucinating, of course. Probably effects of the anesthetic, perhaps not enough was administered to suppress a dream.

I was rather astonished at this out-of-hand dismissal, so I pressed them further. I confessed to never having come across anything precisely about anesthetic insufficiency in the matter of NDEs. I also casually mentioned that my impression of the hallucinations literature—a literature with which I was quite familiar—was that it did not sufficiently cover the NDE.

There was a short silence, a couple sips of wine, then finally one of my lunch companions self-consciously, if rather gaily, leered at me. "Come, come, Allan. Don't tell me you want us to believe that the dead exist and that they are just waiting around surgical theaters all over the world to reacquaint themselves with the living!"

What fabulously hilarious lunch companions I had that day. So, to indulge myself with colleagues who, because of our friendliness, would indeed indulge me, I pushed on through the noontime hilarity. Just give me, I petitioned them, one single reference that was an empirical study and not a piece of neurological theory about how near-death visitors are hallucinations. Just give me the citation that I can look up for myself.

And of course they did not have a single reference to offer. In the face of religious intolerance and an overweaned confidence in a material view of the world, they assumed that there *must be* such a study. But there was not such a study in 1983 when I had this exchange, and there is not such a study in 2019 as I write these words.

So in this chapter we will survey the body of research around hallucinations, the brain, and perceptions. What do we know, and what may we never know? And we will ask how genuinely useful is the descriptor *hallucination*. Does it help us understand these experiences in terms of patient psychology, our patient-family-doctor communications, or even for just sheer causal explanations?

I argue that the term *hallucination* is not all that useful for understanding unusual perceptions at the end of life. It is not helpful in managing clinical relations with patients and families, and it is not very good as a basic explanation. It does not explain most of the major unusual perceptions observed near death. Please note my emphasis on the term *argument*, because these are arguments—deductions from the existing scientific literature.

That all visions of the dead are hallucinations is also an argument. By rehearsing my particular argument here, I am creating an intellectual space for a perspective that we rarely hear. The most common hallucination argument is itself rarely examined, while the so-called alternative arguments are viewed as merely religious or unserious. Here, in this chapter, I offer an anthropological or sociological viewpoint that considers the hallucination argument but sets limits to its generalizability as defined even by the very field itself.[1] This is not a religious argument, because I am not interested in demonstrating the "reality" of the afterlife but rather the reality of how these visitations are important dimensions of our social lives past, present, and future.

Seeing and Hearing What Is "Not There"

Unusual perceptions—sometimes more formally known as *idiosyncratic perceptions* or *pseudo-hallucinations*[2]—are perceptions of objects or experiences that seem to have no objective reality.[3] Sometimes these are similar to outright hallucinations, that is, "perceptual experiences in the absence of external stimuli that is sufficiently compelling to be considered a true perception."[4] The difference is unusual perceptions have no underlying evidence of organic pathology or psychopathology. There is some debate over whether idiosyncratic perceptions are a subcategory of hallucinations or that it is hallucinations that are the subcategory of idiosyncratic perceptions.[5] The epidemiological evidence tends to support the latter, that hallucinations are a diagnostic subcategory of idiosyncratic perceptions.

Although precise estimates concerning the prevalence of idiosyncratic perceptions in the normal population vary widely, they tell a similar story about their sizable significance: one study found that between 0.6 and 84 percent of people will experience one in a lifetime;[6] another placed the number between 4 and 25 percent;[7] a third between 5 and 15 percent;[8] a fourth between 10 and 15 percent;[9]

a fifth found a median prevalence depending on subsample variation (class, ethnicity, country) of 13 percent;[10] and a sixth about 12 percent in developing countries.[11] Yes, these studies have come up with some radically different numbers, yet all of them agree on one thing: far from being rare, these experiences are impressively common.

The variations to the prevalence data above are due to the use of different definitions, methodologies, or populations. Even when idiosyncratic perceptions are narrowly viewed as part of a first-occurrence psychotic experience, the prevalence is about 7 percent, and only about 20 percent of those will suffer a more psychotic experience. Eighty percent of even these will remit over time.[12] In this epidemiological context, the particular type of hallucinations attributable to serious mental disorders (such as bipolar or schizophrenia) is extremely small compared with the general population prevalence figures overall for idiosyncratic or pseudo-hallucinatory perceptions. That is, way more people experience unusual perception than have serious mental disorders.

In general, and it is important to stress this, the key epidemiological fact is that the prevalence figures for idiosyncratic perceptions are the social norm and not the psychopathic ones. Most people who see and hear things that others cannot see or hear will never see a psychiatrist or psychiatric hospital. People see and hear things that others do not, and it does not mean they are crazy, on drugs, or going insane. Still, some dissenters see this normal group as suspicious, arguing instead that these kinds of populations should be viewed as part of a "psychotic continuum"—from prone to persistent to impairment.[13]

The prevalence of hallucinations at the end of life depends on not merely the diagnosis but also the pharmacotherapy given to the dying person. For example, the cross-sectional prevalence of hallucinations in those with Parkinson's disease is about 50 percent, with a cumulative frequency nearing 83 percent toward the end stages of the disease.[14] About half of these hallucinations are visual.[15]

Some 12 to 53 percent of those with dementia experience hallucination depending on the type,[16] but in Alzheimer's disease the rise in incidence of hallucinations is linked to rapid decline.[17]

Although early estimates of the prevalence of hallucinations in patients in hospice care were small (about 1 percent),[18] Dr. Averil Fountain argued this was mainly due to underreporting by patients who feared being classified as mentally ill.[19] Fountain's own survey of British palliative inpatients found the prevalence of hallucinations to be 47 percent—and about half of these were related to sleep. Although Fountain argued that polypharmacy (taking a number of drugs together) was a significant risk factor for all hospice patients, there was only a weak link associating hallucinations with opioid use and the number of drugs prescribed. Most importantly, she was unable to explain why nonhallucinators, who took a similar number and type of drugs as hallucinators, did not hallucinate.

From the brief overview of prevalence figures reviewed earlier, we can see that as an observer moves away from the social psychiatry of normal experience into patient populations with organic changes, high psychoactive pharmacy use, and psychopathology, the term *hallucination* is more and more often deployed. It is in this specialized context that palliative medicine finds itself—servicing mainly a cancer-specific population with high levels of depression and anxiety and frequent use of psychoactive pharmacy. Could any of these be the cause?

Although depression is common in people battling cancer (15–50 percent)[20] and individuals often suffer major depressive episodes, these episodes are not highly associated with hallucinations (less than 1 percent).[21] On the other hand, delirium is very common in palliative patients (upward of 85 percent), but the symptoms and content of this kind of hallucination are highly diverse, invariably stressful to the patient, and attended by negative emotions, disorganized thinking, and disorientation.[22]

There are also minor hallucinations that can be distressing but are well recognized as common in hospice—light flashes or vague shapes reported by patients with migraines, brain tumors, or eye disease.[23] They may also experience hypnogogic (occurring right before falling asleep) or hypnopompic (occurring right after waking up) perceptions of living persons whom they know. And into this environment enter a subgroup of patients and their families who report particularly unusual or idiosyncratic perceptions but with a consistent set of visual imagery, mostly experienced as positive. The two most common and controversial examples are NDEs and deathbed visions (DBVs), but, as we discussed earlier, they may not stop with patients. The bereaved also report unusual perceptions after the death of loved ones.

NDEs, as we have seen, are accounts from patients who were near death but recovered from coma or some other medical crisis.[24] Many of these people subsequently describe idiosyncratic perceptions of out-of-body experiences, tunnel sensation, meeting deceased friends or relatives, or communing with a being of light or similar supernatural figure, usually in some pleasant, heaven-like environment. The prevalence of this type of experience/perception is conservatively estimated to be around 10 percent.[25]

On the other hand, DBVs are simply idiosyncratic perceptions reported by the dying some hours or even days before death.[26] In these reports, the dying may describe appearances by deceased friends and relatives at the bedside. They will often hold conversations with the deceased and report that the deceased are "calling" to them. Overwhelmingly, however counterintuitive this might seem to readers unfamiliar with this literature or experience, those near death report that these perceptions and experiences are positive, pleasant, and comforting. The prevalence of this type of idiosyncratic perception has been estimated to be as low as 10 percent in a study of hospice patients in the United Kingdom.[27]

However, my own studies conducted in India[28] and the Republic of Moldova[29] suggest that the UK prevalence is an underestimation. Prevalence in the Indian and Moldovan studies is as high as 30 percent. The key observation, aside from any cultural considerations,[30] is that the median time of reports of appearances of DBVs by the dying from both the Indian and Moldovan studies appears to be two days before the event of death. The UK study conducted its census some ten days before death, and so this might account for the major discrepancy in estimated prevalence rates.

After the death, the presiding palliative care physician or the bereavement service of the hospital or hospice will conduct a bereavement follow-up. In these interviews, the bereaved often report unusual perceptions. These will commonly include encounters with a "sensed presence," conversations, even full-blown appearances of the deceased. These do not conform to any standard definition of hallucination or pseudo-hallucination,[31] and many clinicians consider these normal experiences.[32] Moreover, the prevalence of this type of perception is very high. One study placed it at 30 percent,[33] another placed it at 49 percent,[34] a third placed it at 80 percent,[35] and a fourth, in Japan, placed it at 90 percent.[36]

Of all the hallucinations, whether organic or pharmaceutically induced, that we encounter in palliative medicine, it is these latter examples—NDEs, DBVs, and visions of the bereaved (VBs)[37]—that seem exceptional. Unlike most hallucinations, and similar to most idiosyncratic perceptions in the general population, these particular perceptions are neither negative nor distressing. The visitors seen in these experiences are viewed as supportive, offering information or truths that are credible to the reasonable-minded, tend to enhance personal and social functioning, and tend not to be associated with organic brain disorders.[38] Yet these subgroups of perceptions in health care are commonly classified as hallucinations by academics and clinicians.

For example, out-of-body experiences are commonly viewed as dissociative experiences.[39] Some researchers have asserted that each particular feature—out-of-body experiences, tunnel sensations—can be understood as its own hallucination.[40] These perceptions have also been linked to epilepsy and to the organic changes and characteristics of this particular disorder.[41] Some neuroscience writers have linked some of the near-death phenomenology to experiments that have deliberately elicited similar experiences such as bright lights, tunnel sensations, or memories of the dead.[42] These experiences have been linked with neurological theories about hallucination causation in cases of epilepsy, Parkinson's disease, or Alzheimer's disease. The positive emotions experienced within these have been linked to pharmacotherapy at the end of life or to the body's own dopamine or opioid systems.

Not only are these technical attempts to sweep idiosyncratic perceptions near death into the narrow remit of psychopathology, but they are also fundamentally awkward scientific explanations in themselves. Even worse, by hastily psychopathologizing these phenomena, we encourage a response toward the dying and their families that may be both misguided (to themselves and the people under their care) and unfounded.

There are two important decision points when one might diagnose a hallucination. The first decision must be made in the face of the prevalence figures concerning hallucinations, because this shows us how likely it is that a person is hallucinating. Since most idiosyncratic perceptions are not indications of psychopathology and are unlikely to progress to such, the decision to ascribe the term *hallucination* to idiosyncratic perceptions near death is rather puzzling and contrary. Second, if one goes against the stronger likelihood and diagnoses a hallucination, will the relevant studies support such a diagnosis? Will it offer us better certainty and a firmer foundation for therapeutic action than not diagnosing? The short answer to these questions is no.

The Limitations of Hallucination Research

In basic epistemological terms—deciding what constitutes certain facts so that we can decide what constitutes true or false propositions in relation to that body of knowledge—most of us think about hallucinations as an established line of scientific inquiry.

For example, a botanist who distinguishes a cactus from any other flowering plant does so on the basis of certain basic organographic criteria: the cactus has aeroles (a woolly base supporting a spine), the seed has two cotyledons, the fruit is a berry enclosing a one-cell seed, they are perennials, and the flower always arises from the top of the ovary. These five criteria together distinguish cacti from other flowering plants.[43] However, even this basic way of thinking about facts cannot be applied to the study of hallucinations. This is the first major reality check against lightly choosing to describe a perception or experience as a hallucination.

There are major theoretical problems with the definition of hallucinations, a term heavily and heatedly contested for the past two hundred years.[44] Philosophers, forensic psychologists, and criminal case lawyers have consistently argued that perception is not simply a vehicle whose function is the receipt of objective images from the environment where such perceptions can be reliably supported by other witnesses. This view has been called *naive realism*.[45] The central factors in perception are not objects or experiences in themselves but rather the expectations and preconceptions we bring to them.[46] Unusual perceptions and experiences that meet most clinical criteria for hallucination are widely prevalent in the general population who mostly appear perfectly functional.[47] Consider these common examples: the visions of charismatic and Pentecostal Christians, the imaginary friends of children, the experiences of the bereaved, and the inner voice of conscience or inspiration.[48] This is why many psychiatrists claim, rather more cautiously, that hallucinations are perhaps best viewed as a symptom,[49] like a cough,[50] a common experience that may or may not lead to psychopathology.

In fact, unusual or idiosyncratic perceptions are so common and apparently so pleasurable that around the world and for all of recorded time people have deliberately been inducing them in religious and recreational contexts—often culturally sanctioned contexts.[51] We see these examples from holy sites like Lourdes and Fatima to peyote rituals among the Mexican Indians to the recreational use of psychoactive substances today.

The definitional problems invariably lead to major clinical problems in differential diagnosis and management. Hallucinations cannot help distinguish between neurotic disorders and psychotic ones.[52] Even within the copious literature on hallucinations based on studies of schizophrenia, the construct of schizophrenia itself has been shown to have poor reliability and validity. Two people can receive the same diagnosis without having any symptoms in common.[53] The mere presence of hallucinations *does not* predict mental health deterioration or progression into professional help. The biggest factor that predicts and leads to clinical attention and scrutiny is the personal reaction to these unusual perceptions—whether a person feels he or she has lost personal control and needs professional help.[54]

Simply looking for psychological or environmental triggers for hallucinations does not inspire confidence either. Many of these so-called triggers seem contradictory, even absurd. People are likely to develop hallucinations when alone, when in crowds, when socially withdrawn, or during social engagements.[55] Some studies say hallucinations may be associated with post-traumatic stress disorder.[56] Some studies say they may not.[57] Some studies found they can be prompted by religious adherence and belief; others found that religious belief and adherence protected subjects from risk of hallucination.[58]

There are two unresolved contradictions that crisscross the field of hallucination studies. First, the main cognitive and psychodynamic theories of hallucination fit awkwardly in a pharmacological model, which has had some success managing hallucinations of a psychopathologic or organic origin, especially those working with the dopamine hypothesis.[59] Second, although the psychiatric definitions of delusions, illusions, and hallucinations are precise and clear, they are not supported by similarly discrete physiological signatures in stereoelectroencephalograph studies.[60]

There are similarly serious deficiencies in imaging studies. Functional magnetic resonance imaging studies have demonstrated that idiosyncratic perceptions of clinical and nonclinical ("normal") populations seem to have similar neural mechanisms. But we do not know why these are experienced so differently by their respective percipients.[61] Or consider button-press studies. These are studies that ask patients to press a button when they feel the onset of a hallucination. But these may capture only the motor response. The auditory-active parts of the brain may be reading the scanner noise rather than the auditory hallucinations. Also, patient recruitment and needs assessment are not consistent across studies, and a substantial number of studies fail to control for the effects of medication (especially antipsychotics) on neural activity.[62] To make matters worse, comparative studies of nonclinical populations have been small in number—as few as nine participants—and, for the most part, small in sample sizes.[63]

Despite the confidence of some researchers in neuroimaging, there is actually very limited anatomical specificity to many hallucinatory states. In 2009, researchers observed that repeated seizures or the stimulation of a single area of the brain in a patient can produce many different types of hallucinations.[64] And conversely, repeated stimulation of widely different areas of the brain can produce surprisingly similar phenomena.

The many theories of cortical "irritation," excitability or release, "top-down" activity, dream or memory intrusion, or misperception, for all their creative diversity, do not fully account for hallucinations or their diversity.[65] They all come down to a rather general and modest explanation about neural connectivity or suppression, and this, in the end, is a vague and imprecise set of facts[66] that is not even enough for a botanist to distinguish a cactus.

To illustrate how limited and unhelpful current hallucination research is in attempting to understand unusual experiences of those who are near death, let me provide some brief examples of academics explaining the NDE. In a 2011 article, subtitled "How Neuroscience Can Explain Seeing Bright Lights, Meeting the Dead, or Being Convinced You Are One of Them," the authors list a few explanations. Among them, the authors assert that an "awareness" of "being dead" is the patient's own attempt to "make sense of strange experiences the patient is having."[67] This is not a neuroscience explanation. They also assert that out-of-body experiences are brain-based sensations and can be simulated by stimulation of parts of the brain. Unfortunately, the methodological axiom operative here is that electrical or hypnotic simulation does not mean the experiences they resemble are not in fact real. Sensations and perceptions of sexual intercourse or traveling on a train can be simulated, but that does not mean that sex or train travel does not exist in the real world.[68]

Early anthropological studies demonstrated that tunnel sensations in near-death reports are not cross-cultural.[69] The problem here, then, is that some researchers develop universal neuroscience models for behavior and experience before checking the transcultural psychiatric and anthropological data that suggests some of the phenomenology is culture specific. The same can be said about the claim that most of the perceptions reported by those near death can be attributed to cerebral anoxia—oxygen starvation in the brain.[70] This is an academically blinkered claim that ignores the abundant and long-standing evidence of fully conscious people who are not near death and yet report identical perceptual phenomenology.[71]

Finally, the article attributes seeing the dead to misperception, externally ascribed sources, or "over-activation" in "brain structures." The article uses examples from cases of organic brain disorder such as Parkinson's disease or Alzheimer's disease, even though near-death cases have no significant association with these diagnostic categories. There is no explanation given as to why, in the absence of significant clinical populations with psychopathology among those who are near death,[72] psychopathology models are nevertheless employed as relevant constructs. Most people who are near death are neurologically normal, so why employ psychopathological models?

Some researchers argue that each of the features of NDEs—tunnel sensation, life review, and bright lights—can be accounted for as individual hallucinations.[73] But there are no empirical studies to support this claim. They even postulate a "genetic prearrangement," but no genetics-based studies about NDEs are available.

And what about the good emotions, the feelings of enveloping warmth and love within these NDEs? Some researchers link them to pharmacotherapies (drugs and especially painkillers) administered at the end of life or to the body's own dopamine or opioid systems. Reviews of first-person accounts of the dying experience across cultures and history[74] have demonstrated that positive emotions during life-limiting illness and near death are as common as negative emotions, and they can occur at any time in the dying process, even long before painkillers—whether the body's own or administered—would be necessary. To reach for solely biological or pharmacological explanation for positive or negative human emotions during crisis, as commonly found in the rest of life itself, is academic overgeneralization at best and reductionism at its worst.

Hallucination theories do not help us decide whether hallucinations are necessarily indicative of psychosis or neurosis. They cannot help us make reasonable differential diagnoses. And they cannot even point us to the underlying neuromechanism for most perceptual irregularities.[75] Hallucination as a construct is of little to no use to us as an academic explanation or as a source of clinical guidance for unusual perceptions at the end of life where no obvious underlying organic or psychiatric etiology is apparent. Labeling NDEs, DBVs, or VBs as hallucinations is unhelpful at best, and at worst it is stigmatizing and alarming for patients and families—all without even the benefit of recommending any specific type of support.

The Place of Biography and Culture at the End of Life

It is not the purpose of this chapter to dismiss all current and past research into hallucinations. But despite popular impressions to the contrary, the field currently offers only elementary insights for highly specific syndromes and discrete problems. Nevertheless, the diagnosis of hallucinations is widely employed—even by those outside the field of hospice care—to generalize other perceptual experiences and problems.

To make matters worse, research designs from the field of hallucination studies borrow from multiple and often clashing epistemologies: pharmacology, neurology, neuropsychology, psychiatry, psychoanalysis, and cognitive psychology. These circumstances give rise to sharp differences in observation, language, theory construct, and findings. The findings with the strongest clinical promise are those where organic changes to the brain are better understood (e.g., in epilepsy, Charles Bonnet Syndrome, or Parkinson's disease) or where there has been a long tradition of research with a particular example of psychopathology (e.g., psychotic disorders). Arising from these conclusions about the limits to the current study of hallucinations are two implications that are pertinent for care at the end of life in palliative medicine.

The first implication is the importance of acknowledging the limits to any application of constructs from the field of hallucination studies, as these might apply to any unusual experiences at the end of life that are not prima facie linked to organic pathology or psychopathology. The actual experimental or empirical study (as opposed to speculative study) of unusual perceptions of this type near death is simply not available. The hasty application of psychopathological models to explain these unusual perceptions raises the suspicion that the attempts are designed to respond in a dismissive way to popular spiritual and religious interests rather than being an expression of impartial scientific curiosity. Since these unusual perceptions are often perceptions that appear not to disturb personal or social function at the end of life, they fall rather logically into the realm of "normal" experiences of idiosyncratic perceptions.

The second, but somewhat more troublesome, implication of this review is to ask what can be learned from the study of hallucinations, with all its current limitations, that is useful to those of us working with unusual perceptions at the end of life.

We must acknowledge that hallucinations are cross-cultural, because psychopathology and dysfunctional organic changes to the brain can happen to anybody, anywhere. For most people, however, for most of the time, idiosyncratic perceptions are not best explained by mental illness. A recent major review of interdisciplinary approaches to hallucinations[76] showed that the research emphases in the field have stressed the use of scales and measures and the significance of pathology.[77] But the actual content of unusual perceptions is largely underresearched. Also unexplored is the role of unusual perceptions in normal individuals undergoing personal change and crisis and the potential good uses of these perceptions.[78] Theorizing the "normal" from the workaday world of the clinic has been an occupational hazard that has led to "exposure bias"—a bias that has fostered the habit of seeing all unusual perceptions through the lens of pathology rather than health and well-being.[79]

Yet, in hospice care, it is precisely these areas concerning the quality of psychological and social experience, the cycle of crisis and change, and the support of well-being over curative measures that are hallmarks of this type of care. As one study observed as early as 1995, therapeutic interventions that "do not negotiate with patient meanings of culturally sanctioned hallucinations tend to fail in their treatments."[80] Taking seriously the patient content of unusual perceptual experiences creates three positive spaces for the patient-family-doctor relationship. First, it requires all parties to jointly establish whether these perceptions are to be expected because they resemble ones known to be associated with certain diagnostic categories or diseases, like Alzheimer's or Parkinson's. Second, it steers the clinician away from an unhelpful diagnosis of hallucination made as a "diagnosis of exclusion." This often-premature diagnosis limits rather than encourages a clinical openness toward alternative and sometimes unconventional hypotheses for the source of these experiences. Some of these will have discernible or discoverable possibilities, and some will not.

For example, the sources of some unusual voice perceptions turned out not to be hallucinations but rather radio transmissions from dental fillings, shrapnel, or hearing aids.[81] Furthermore, at the end of the day, when other sources for unusual perceptions remain hidden or inexplicable, the best clinical and scientific advice may be to adopt humility before the data. In 2010, one study reported a case of a woman who heard an "inner voice" that urged her to seek treatment and a brain scan and even directed her to a hospital. After obeying "her voice," she was found to have a benign meningioma, which was subsequently removed by surgery. After the surgery the voice bid her farewell and never recurred. Reflecting on this case, the study's author, J. M. Pierre, observed, "This controversial case reminds us of the potential for seemingly unlimited interpretation of auditory hallucination by patients and clinicians alike."[82]

In these curious but not infrequent cases, when the pendulum of the unusual swings back toward the broader experiences of the everyday, we do well to look to the humanities and social sciences. These investigative traditions take the diversity of "subjective data" arising from cultural norms as their major subject of study rather than a focus on the strange and deviant. Jennifer Windt, of Johannes Gutenberg University,[83] citing William James,[84] describes a set of experiences that, at least taxonomically, comes close to what we observe in these visions near death or during bereavement: intellectual enlightenment or satisfaction, elation, and sometimes joy, all apprehended in immediate experience rather than rational deliberation, difficulty in communicating the experience to others, and woefully difficult to distinguish from delusions. These characteristics have often been described by anthropologists and religious studies scholars as "mystical experience."

At this point in the chapter, we arrive at the borderlands of psychiatry and religion and their intersection within culture and biography.[85] Similar to the field of hallucination studies, these different perspectives offer up potentially clashing ways of seeing the world. Whether we choose loaded phrases such as *mystical experiences*, *pseudo-hallucinations*, or *paranormal perceptions*, we can nevertheless agree on three overlapping observations.[86] One, that these kinds of perceptions are really justified only by first-person experience. They rarely have any public witness or support. Two, these experiences do not seem disprovable by current neuroscience theory or experiment. They seem, by most philosophical accounts, to lie outside the scope of epistemology, the basic assumptions about what constitutes real knowledge. And three, the question of whether these experiences really do give rise to deeper forms of knowledge may be unanswerable.

Such characteristic experiences have been the foundation of religious knowledge and belief in the past, and today they fuel the religious and spiritual beliefs of many others outside of formal religious institutions. It is not for medicine to contribute to or to detract from this relationship, because there is no scientific or clinical basis for doing either. Instead, this brief review of the field of hallucinations studies leaves us with more pressing questions: If we are not to fall into the traditional traps of naive realism or character assassination—using pathological models to explain nonpathological behavior and perception—how might we view the abnormal normal perception? Are there any other realities to consider between "reality" and "hallucination"?

The answers lie in understanding the *social nature* of normal perception, interpretation, and experience. Though there is a basic material order in the world, it is, however, important to acknowledge that this is indeed a very *basic* order and that most perceptual knowledge depends on personal experience and social context. To understand *how* we see, we must understand our usual *ways* of seeing. Although you and I may see a tomato in the kitchen, the reasons why you say "tom-may-to" but I say "tom-mah-to" raise not only the issue of why we describe the same thing differently but also (and more intriguingly) the question about whether we are actually seeing the same thing. In the next chapter, we will look at that proposition a bit more closely.

3

Perception

WHEN I WAS six years old my father asked me to go on an errand. I was greatly pleased by this request. My former attempts to complete errands on behalf of my parents had been a litany of failure and disappointment for all parties. Either I would bring home the wrong item, I would bring too many or not enough items, or I would simply not come home at all, forgetting at some point why I had gone out that day, meeting friends, and going off to enjoy myself with them. This latest request, I reasoned, was another opportunity to prove to my parents that I could *eventually* do the job properly.

My father was a smoker. He pushed some money into my hands and said, "Son, go down to the corner store and buy me a pack of Camels."

I left immediately, as though I had been shot out of a circus cannon. As I walked along the street, steely-eyed and determined not to forget the object of my journey, I kept repeating the name: "Camels." Passersby could hear me muttering as I walked past them. "Camels . . . Camels . . . Camels."

Finally, I reached the store and turned into the doorway. I could see a very large man behind the counter. He leaned toward me as I entered and asked in a deep gruff voice, "How can I help you?"

At that point, I felt a momentary sensation of nausea and euphoria, and I leaned toward him and asked cheerily, "Could I have a pack of donkeys?"

The resulting exchange happened rapidly and had the character of mutual panic. He said he had no donkeys. I said he must be hiding them. He said I must be mistaken. I said I could not be mistaken or else my father would not have sent me to collect them. He said that was ridiculous. I said I had no idea what that meant. There was a brief silence as we both drew breath.

There was no more to be said. Communication had completely failed us at that point. I turned to go home, again empty-handed.

When I reached home my father asked me, "Why did you ask for donkeys?" A good question.

Not long after I left the store, as I began to calm down, I realized what I had actually said to the shop owner. I was supposed to ask for camels—to me a strange but inexplicably appealing animal. I began to think why—*how*—I had managed to ask for donkeys when I "knew" I was supposed to ask for camels.

So when my father asked his forensic question, I offered him the only answer that made any sense to me: "I like donkeys an awful lot!"

At six I realized that I had what I would later be able to better describe as a bias. My love of donkeys, in a moment of high anxiety and stress, had obliterated my temporary but highly focused attention on camels and expunged both that image and word from my brain at the crucial moment. Just when I needed it the most, *camel* deserted my mind and was replaced by *donkeys*. I was not deluded or hallucinating. I was mistaken, yes. Confused, surely. But the bias was obvious and explained both my error and the enthusiasm with which I energetically defended it. This happens all the time, and on more serious topics than merely remembering the right brand of cigarettes.

People make perceptual mistakes in all settings because of their biases. And the key reason is not because they are occasionally "wrong" in their perceptions or their thinking but rather because the problem of bias is integral to normal thinking and perceiving. As sociologists would say, it is only broad social consensus that keeps multiple individual biases from impeding everyday life. Our mistake is to think bias is an odd or occasional event—it is really our modus operandi. Biases are reined in and managed by social conventions. It is only when these "conventions"—norms, customs, rites, shared assumptions—fail or momentarily relax their grip that particular instances of bias become noticeable to others.

Societies develop rules, norms, and even ideologies about the nonnegotiable aspects of everyday life so that each new encounter with most physical and social products and situations does not have to be reinvented. We all learn the way things are. We come to agree on the ways of the world, its colors, objects, topographies, words, and customs. We see just how important these are when we see how new immigrants struggle with even the simplest meanings and customs that we take for granted about our own society.

The built-in biases we carry inside us are created by the specifics of personality and place. This means that eccentric individuals can be quickly labeled mentally disordered, outsiders, or criminals. Their "biases" consistently flout the rules and threaten the social and moral order, the way things are. Either they refuse to have their individual perceptions reined in or moderated, or they cannot see or read the need to do this based on the everyday "social contract" we share with each other about how to behave.

So, the reason why some "see" and "hear" things others do not is because they "come" from a different place. This observation is obvious, and that is why it is commonly overlooked. Because we each occupy a different place as individuals, with different abilities and flaws and backgrounds that shape our bias one way and not another way, we therefore consequentially and logically see different things.

The meaning of the term *place* here is important because it is not only meant to indicate a difference in geography, for instance, American, British, African, Japanese. It also means a social place, like a tall person or a short person, a woman or a man, a child or an adult, or a white person or a person of color. And then there are cultural places: religious background, family background, educational or class background, being twelve as opposed to ninety-two. These meanings represent places—positions and perspectives in the world that shape our biases. Just as sitting on top of a hill gives you a different view and experience from those at the base, so too does social and cultural position change our individual perceptions of the physical world.

This chapter is about the sociology and subjectivity of perception. These opening remarks are the foundational idea of both modern sociology and the modern psychology of perception. Not recognizing that different perceptions of "reality" are normal leads us too quickly to turn to topics in abnormal psychology, like hallucination theories—why should we believe that significant divergence of experience and interpretation must be sought from abnormal psychology rather than normal psychology?

Tom-may-to, Tom-mah-to

Consider this important but constantly overlooked fact about the very human nature of perception: there is a lot of ground between the idea of so-called hallucinations and so-called reality. This makes sense if you think about it for a moment. There is a lot of variation between hating someone and falling in love with them. Between being "right" and being "wrong" about a decision there is much that is a "little" or "a bit more" or "a lot" right or wrong about it. You might believe that you made a right decision but look back later and believe that it was wrong. Binary thinking is an oversimplification in relationships and life in general, so it should be no surprise that the same cautions apply when we speak about "reality" or "hallucination."

Let us briefly remind ourselves of the many ways in which this plays out in our everyday life. There are several examples that illustrate why—in normal and everyday experience, any one person will see a particular thing and another will not.

Consider tests for color blindness. A significant proportion of the population anywhere is color-blind. This is caused by a genetic condition that affects the light-sensitive cells at the back of the eye. Many people grow up with color blindness and do not know they have it until the condition is found through eye tests. Both color-blind people and those who are not color-blind will have perceptual experiences that are unremarkable to them *until* they compare notes of what the other sees. Before and even after the awareness of the differences, it is clear that some things that can be seen by those who are color-blind cannot be seen by those who are not. Conversely, some things seen by those who are not color-blind cannot be seen by those who are. In the case of color perception, we often see color blindness as "abnormal" due to genetic defect. But physical differences such as color blindness may not be pathological—they may simply be differences due to genetic inheritance just like any other trait, like height, touch perception, sexual arousal, or hearing acuity. And there is a large range of these differences, some that bestow serious differences in perception and some only slight differences. That's life. Just because I see colors or have sensations of touch quite different from you does not make my experiences (or yours) "hallucinatory." The abnormal in this instance is simply physical difference bestowing equally different advantages and disadvantages.

There are individual differences of perception linked to individual differences in genetic or organic makeup, but there are also differences in *ways of seeing things*. Stereograms or Magic Eye puzzles that were popular in the 1990s are a very good example of this. Presented with a picture that simply looks like a series of patterned repetitions, we are asked to stare at this pattern for so long that eventually we will see an image beneath the pattern. At first the pattern will look like a series of wavy lines or scribbles, but eventually it will morph into a 3D image, and suddenly we will see a shark swimming beneath the sea or the Statue of Liberty.

The bad news for some is that regardless of how long they stare at the picture they will never see the shark or the statue. Some will see it only if they are schooled to see it—given techniques to blur the image. You are not being trained to hallucinate. You are, however, being shown how to view a piece of reality in another way. Reality, in this example, is more than what it seems at first. It is not a simple case of letting the light from the image enter our eye and—presto—we see the shark. We must retune our eyes to see other aspects of the light from the image.

Magic Eye puzzles are part of a broader class of optical illusions. If you have ever taken a first-year course in introductory psychology, you would have been exposed to these very quickly. There are a number of old and very famous optical illusions, where the first impressions are inaccurate or misleading or continue to change even while you look at them. The mind plays tricks with shapes.[1] In other words, the mind follows rules about how objects should look and behave. If these objects are slightly altered, the mind tends to distort them to make them fit into the rules. The result is a distortion of the image. This is why many people simply cannot see things unless they are shown how. Many people's perception routine simply deletes images that are before them but unacceptable to their own rules about what to see.

We often forget or, worse, take for granted the self-evident nature of seeing and overlook that it is both retrieving data from the material world and simultaneously imposing information on that

Perception

incoming data. Our conclusions about what we are seeing are mostly biased in favor of the view that it is incoming data that is important, and a simultaneously common denial of what we impose on that information to make our conclusions.

This is why so-called eyewitnesses in a court of law require interrogation. Witnesses do not simply report what they saw but more often what they believe they saw, often unable or unwilling to disentangle the two. It is up to lawyers to strip the testimony back to the facts. Perception is selective. We notice what grabs our attention, but our attention is biased toward events, actions, or objects that are attractive to us or that worry or threaten us. We tend not to notice things that have no relevance to us—I could not tell you the color of the carpet in the shop where I asked for donkeys. That is why when students are asked to drive around the block in a car and report everything they see, they can never answer the question, How many telephone poles did you pass? It is a common experiment proving subjective perception to ask students to watch a video of a gang fight. Afterward, students are asked who had the knife. In the melee, it is hard to see much of anything specific. Often the students report that a black gang member had the knife. But in fact, the video contained no knife at all.

These examples show biased perception. The first example shows how people do not see things that are actually there. The second example shows how they see things that are not there. But there is more. We know from ethnological studies that some early cultures had problems "seeing" photographs. We forget that as a culture we grow up learning how to see images in photographs and artwork. In other cultures, without this taken-for-granted socialization, the surface of a photo can simply look like a mash of colors and blobs. For other societies, looking through new technologies (for them) such as binoculars or telescopes can seem to bring animals, humans, or trees suddenly into their presence, right beside them. The amplification of distant images can seem like sudden transportation or teleportation of the objects to their novice viewers. They must learn that visual amplification is not a real movement of the object but merely an appearance of drawing something closer.

All these examples illustrate the key principles of the psychology of perception. Bias is integral and normal to our experience of perception. We must recognize that "attention" means focus and bias. To attend to something is to select one piece of environmental information over a myriad of competing possibilities and then attribute meaning to it and integrate it into other meaning systems. For example, to look for cauliflower in the supermarket, find it, choose the best one, check it off the mental shopping list, and move to the next item.[2]

Perception and the Manufacturing of Sense

Although most people think there is a "self-evident" relationship between the physical environment and what they see, the actual technical reality is that all we are really aware of is psychological experience. "Brain activity" is not another phrase for perception. The brain processes perception, meaning that it selects, manages, and imposes meanings and therefore rearranges everything you perceive. Without a doubt our ears, eyes, skin, tongue, and nose receive input from the outside world, but at the same time our brain tampers with that information as it attempts to sort colors, sounds, taste, pain, and pleasure. These qualities of experience must make sense. To say it another way, we "make sense" of the world rather than merely "receive sense." A raised heart rate and respiration rate accompanied by sweaty palms and a sense of giddiness may be the beginnings of a panic attack, or it might be the pleasurable excitement one feels before stepping up to a podium to receive an award. It is we who "make" the sense, who make the senses make sense.[3] "Literal physical stimulus is nothing like your perceptual experience. Electromagnetic energy contains no psychological meaning."[4]

Perception

Not only does environmental stimuli need processing by our psychological system, but there is a physical limit to our ability to process incoming data. We are continuously flooded by data. Memory holds the data during and immediately after cessation of the stimulus, but two things happen during these everyday events. First, most data does not make sense all by itself and needs us to "make sense" of it; this takes time. Second, because making sense of the data takes time, much of the data we receive decays, and decays rapidly. This necessarily means that much perception is missed because of selective attention and pattern recognition biases within our system.[5]

We can break up the idea of normal perception into what psychologists call "bottom-up" and "top-down" processes. The psychologist Bruce Goldstein illustrates this with a story of a woman named Ellen walking in the woods. As Ellen walks along the trail in the woods she is bombarded by perception—things to see, feel, smell, and hear. Her perceptual system scans and selects and she "notices" a particular tree and then a pattern on the tree's trunk. At first she thinks it is moss but then realizes it is a moth. The light rays reflected on the moth create an image in her eye, which results in electrical signals to her brain. This sequence of events is called *bottom-up processing*. Her ability to sort the data she receives—not moss but moth, moth but not butterfly—is *top-down processing*.[6]

Recognizing objects has many challenges. Occlusion (place obscured by place position), variation in viewpoint (place view from different places), bias (place not noticed or overly attended because of place value), inattention (place being distracted by other priorities of place), among others, and the nervous system adjusts and adapts as best it can to these challenges through *practice and experience*.[7] Even the physical tendency to control and manage the sheer overwhelming input of data and the challenge of its interpretation are governed by culture—the social place from which one comes. How one interprets signals and signs from the outside world may be subject to bias, but bias is heavily influenced by culture.[8]

The most important points to note about all these anthropological and psychological references and descriptions are as follows: (1) Much data is missed or discarded during bottom-up processes, and this is normal; (2) mistakes are made regularly in top-down processes that make an abundance of false-positive perceptions (believing you have seen things that you did not) and false-negative perceptions (believing that things were not there, that actually were). We know from numerous psychology experiments on millions of hapless college students around the world that these types of errors are not merely restricted to individuals but also apply to group and crowd perceptions. (3) The main way we attempt to overcome these errors of attention and judgment is through practice and experience, and the one thing that mystical experiences do *not* afford most people are precisely those qualities—practice or experience—because they are usually uncommon or irregular, *by definition*.

And finally, on the basis of these routine observations, we must conclude that (4) so-called normal perceptions are notoriously unreliable. Apart from any other examples, this is why most judicial systems require a legion of participants (juries, witnesses, judges, etc.) and arguments to make a judgment about what actually occurred in any one set of crime circumstances. Very few things, events, or experiences are "obvious."

Skeptics often talk about the compulsive tendency of human beings to see connections or meaning in meaningless or random materials or events as "apophenia"[9]—for example, seeing the face of Jesus in the wrinkle patterns of pie pastry or the burn patterns of toast. In this way, skeptics argue that this creative tendency most closely resembles psychosis. In other words, this tendency to overinterpret objects is linked or may be closely associated with the same brain processes seen in pathological perceptions. The dominant way to see our perceptual system is to view it as a system prone to biases and flaws. However, we risk overinterpretation ourselves when we link this tendency to malfunction and imperfection. This phenomenon is not malfunction or imperfection but the simple architecture of normal perception. This is also the point made by Thomas West—the dyslexic writer of best sellers—who in a series of stories about genius in science and art points to the exceptional talent and advantage of dyslexics in creativity and the perceptual advantage that gives them exceptional sight and insight in diverse fields from visual artistry and surgery to reading X-rays and MRIs. Such people can "see what others cannot see."[10] But they are not "malfunctioning"; rather, they are merely employing their differences to their advantage.

These exceptional perceptions are also a sign of sharpness and efficiency that "transforms sensory inputs into understanding and interpreting the current situation in a very fast way in order to generate adequate and goal-leading actions in good time." Although the perceptual system gets a bit lost in simple repetitious data and input, we can generally quickly interpret complex data. In this way, a smile is difficult to interpret, but a box of tomatoes or a motor bike is not.[11]

However—and it is important to emphasize this—the tendency to "see" or "hear" things that are not there (to others) because of mental illness or brain anomaly, and the parallel tendency to do the same by normal healthy individuals are not necessarily linked. This is a common pattern recognition error made by critics and skeptics. This error is best exemplified by examples from convergent evolution. In convergent evolution, two plants or animals might physically resemble each other—for example, English hedgehogs and Australian echidnas, or the African succulent *Euphorbia obesa* and the American cactus *Astrophytum asterias*. Both of these animals and plants look very much like each other so that for non-zoologists and non-botanists they may widely be viewed as biologically linked. But they are not linked, except in the sense that these examples have had similar environmental pressures exerted on them for a very long time and so they have adapted in physically similar ways. However, they are not genetically related. In this same type of comparison, some forms of psychosis may indeed resemble the creative cognitive process of normal individuals, but the outcomes of both have quite different organic lineage. The only thing they have in common is *resemblance,* not *cause.*

The Lands of Dying and Grief

So we know that perception can be influenced by characteristics in our perceptual array, our eyes, touch, height, arousal level, and smell. It can be influenced by the nature of the object itself, how complex it appears to senses unprepared for that complexity. And it can be influenced by biases in our attention that blind us to some things and make us see other things that others may not see.

The experience of dying or grieving can change the physical characteristics of perception through possible alterations in our perceptual machinery—from chronic pain, deprivation, psychological stress, oversleep, or undersleep. It can also bring new social experiences of isolation or withdrawal that come from serious illness or bereavement, circumstances that give us new opportunities to notice the taken-for-granted in our social life and in the objects and spaces around us. And with shifts to the usual cycles of habit in work and play or social support, both dying and grieving people have an unusual opportunity to have their perceptual, social, physical, or intellectual biases undermined or challenged. They spend more time in physical and social spaces to which they are unaccustomed and less time with their usual stimuli. This can mean new learning and new views of their perceptual cues. They may notice "new" things. This is a common self-reported observation of both the dying and the bereaved in their everyday social life.[12] And these things tend to begin gradually.

In the months before her death, a cancer patient named Helen describes the beginning of this shift in perceptions:

I might not be here next month or in two months' time or on my next birthday. You then become much more aware of people, your beloved people around you. You know, my little, my little granddaughter...I keep on hugging and kissing her because I don't know how long I will be able to do that. And your senses are sharpened. Suddenly pink roses are much pinker than they used to be, and the blue sky is bluer than it used to be. And you just observe things in a different way. Most of us take things for granted—that's human nature you know?[13]

During his time in the death camps of Auschwitz, the famous psychotherapist Victor Frankl remembered attending to a dying inmate and listening to some of her final observations: "Pointing through the window... she said, 'This tree here is the only friend I have in this loneliness.... I often talk to this tree.'... Was she delirious? Did she have occasional hallucinations?... I asked her if the tree replied. She answered, 'It said to me, "I am here—I am here—I am life, eternal life."'"[14] Were Helen and Victor Frankl's unnamed patient seeing and hearing things that others could not? Clearly they were, but just as clearly they do not quite meet any practical criteria for hallucination or delirium. Their communications and meaning are quite clear. They are articulate and reflective, intelligent. Somehow, Helen's perceptions of the world around her have sharpened, and she sees that world differently from the more pedestrian and jaded way most of us see it, rather notably different from the way even she used to see the world.

Frankl's patient is communicating with a tree. We might say, rather cynically, that she is really communicating with herself. The messages she is receiving are the messages she is sending her internal self, and in turn projecting onto the tree. The problem with that view—as we have seen in the last few pages of our review—is that this is exactly what normal perception is. Remember that our perceptions are psychological, not unadulterated physical reception.

Frankl's dying patient is doing exactly what Frankl himself is doing while perceiving the situation of his patient. Is his entertainment of the delusion possibility simply itself a judgment based on his own bias as a psychiatrist and someone removed from the person he is observing?

This does not mean there is no objective interpretation or no truth to our observations of events. But it does mean—in the matter of people who undergo seriously different circumstances and unusual emotional experiences—that perceptions, observations, and judgments by those not in that situation will tend to be skeptical, naive, and distancing. And the explanations will tend toward abnormal. This will happen in the first instance simply from unfamiliarity with that social and emotional place. Few of us can imagine the situation of facing our own death.

This was one of Sigmund Freud's most enduring points. In his essay "Thoughts for the Times on War and Death," he describes a man who wrote a letter to his wife: "Darling, if one of us should die before the other, I think I shall move to Paris."[15] It is nearly impossible to imagine our own dying, so when it comes to theorizing what must be happening to those who are—and who report observations that are dissonant with our own everyday experience—those observations must be suspect. We are like the Flat Earth theorists who never leave home and assume the horizon speaks for itself. Any news delivered by Columbus or NASA must be damn lies.

And life-while-dying does not stop at merely sharper, richer perceptions of the physical environment, value clarifications, or whispered exchanges from the natural world. A proportion of dying people report even more sensational perceptions as they move closer to death itself. Those with a couple of days to live may report invisible social encounters at their deathbed, while those who are thrust suddenly into a life-threatening situation (often without warning through accident or surgery) may do the same. Here—gradually or suddenly separated from the usual cycles of a normal social life

Perception

or work, school, recreational pursuits, or social interactions—dying people come to occupy a very new social environment. That "new" social environment may be an operating table or a hospice bed, or it might be serious isolation or a sense of personal crisis and loneliness. For every single one of them, the circumstances and experiences are unique. From here, other perceptions have clearly been made possible.

RECALL FROM THE OPENING chapter of this book the mother in India who spoke about the last twenty-four hours of her eight-year-old daughter's life: "On the day that she died, Anita announced to her mother, in a very matter of fact way, that her late grandmother had come to sit with her. (Her grandmother had died four months previously.) The grandmother would sit beside her and chat, occasionally calling for her."[16] It is not unusual for visitors to be seen at this time, as discussed in the previous chapter. Up to 30 percent of people on their deathbed will report these visitors, and most of them are people known to be dead. What I find most remarkable about these encounters is not that they take place—we have documented these visions for millennia—but that dying people seem to receive these visitors unremarkably or unsurprisingly. If I were lying in bed feeling rather ill, and I was suddenly visited by a friend I knew had been dead for some years, I would be, as they say, gobsmacked. You would not hear the end of it from me. The equanimity of dying people who report this is somewhat astonishing. But a moment's thought reveals this observation to be as naive as reaching too quickly for explanations from abnormal psychology (and incidentally, is a major reason why people *do* reach for such explanations).

First, people are beginning an extraordinary journey. Those living with a life-limiting illness go to a perceptual place where few of us have been. They often experience personal news, procedures, treatments, communications, and interpersonal stresses that have few, if any, precedents in their previous, normal life. They are dying from an incurable illness or have experienced an important personal loss.

While on that journey—in the second place, so to speak—they begin to notice that their usual former experiences of, for instance, color, sound, sights, and interpersonal relations take on a new or richer or more meaningful set of perceptions and experience. Their usual world of perception is evolving. Not only do their experiences feel different but they themselves feel different. This is a common observation by bereaved people. And that is only the stuff they are accustomed to encountering.

Third, out of the seemingly different reception of experiences that are usual and typical come experiences that are not. Being very near to death provides some with an evolving psychology from their changing circumstances and stresses. Remember that we are always talking about a psychology—senses make no sense on their own. We manufacture sense from previous experience and knowledge. If you can remember the past, you are seeing and hearing things that are no longer there and cannot be seen or heard by anyone outside your own head. And that past may not be as you remember it. This makes the idea of seeing and hearing things that are not there technically not without precedent.

Those who report new occupants around their bedside have themselves already been in a new world that is always changing. The problem with my imagined reaction to a visit from a dead friend is that I have not done the parallel imagining or experiential work about the space and place that the dying or bereaved occupy. I am imagining a visit from a dead friend only as my healthy, socially integrated, and engaged usual self. That is rarely what the circumstances are for people two days before their death. Living with an important personal loss often leaves one feeling changed forever. The situation for near-death experiences (NDEs) must also be the same. Those who have had an NDE report feeling *forever* changed by it.

It does seem remarkable that people have reported an out-of-body experience, watching their own resuscitation, or meeting a bright being of light, or watching their life flash before their eyes.

But imagine finding yourself in cardiac arrest but still conscious. Or crushed by a large truck but viewing your crushed body and the rescuers attempting to free it.

Tautology? Maybe. But anthropologically and psychologically that is the perceptual data we must resign ourselves to working with. About 10 percent of people in that situation describe just those circumstances.[17] Whether they are delusional or not, their belief in the reality of those circumstances puts them at the center of a very new and novel perceptual place. Unique circumstances generate unique experiences. And that insight is the basis of the normal psychology of perception. We just need to apply these principles to dying and bereavement.

Too often like Freud's man who wrote a letter to his wife, we cannot imagine, no matter how hard we try, a unique situation we have never encountered. We rely on others who have been there to familiarize us. However, when we look to familiarize ourselves we tend to spend less time dedicating ourselves to understanding the circumstances and more time ogling the outcomes—focusing instead on the new appearance of dead visitors and not on how far and how deeply circumstances and psychology have changed for those who report them. How did they—as people just like us—become receptors of the strange and unusual, without drugs, without madness, and often even without religion?

As I argued in the previous chapter, these visits are unlikely to be hallucinations. And we are all still relatively fresh from the Enlightenment—a time when we disentangled ourselves from religious authority. This makes the current cultural climate very hesitant to embrace a form of mystical explanation that is reminiscent of our earlier theories. If it does not square with public scientific understanding, it is hard to know what we are looking at. If it squares more with St. Augustine than Stephen Hawking, that prospect frightens a lot of people. And I am sorry to report that this book will not help you decide which way to go.

But there is another way to view these experiences.

If it is accepted that, at least in principle, many new perceptions of the dying and the bereaved are functions of equally new physical, social, or medical spaces and experiences and are not hallucinations with pathological organic origins, what stops us from thinking conversely that they are simply seeing what they expect to see? They are near death, or they have lost a loved one—aren't they all searching for an afterlife?

That is a fair question. After all, seeing new things when your physical or social environment has dramatically changed should not be a surprise. Seeing the dead or supernatural might be a big ask, unless that is what you expect to see. Death has a way of prompting the bereaved and the dying to think about, and maybe even expect, something from the beyond.

There are plenty of instances of atheists and skeptics going through NDEs. But that is an easy way to knock this possibility on the head. The bigger problem with this line of thinking is the assumption that expectation and the meeting of that expectation is somehow discrediting. It is like the hypnosis argument. Yes, hypnosis can create or simulate experiences for those near death. It can also simulate sex and train travel, but that does not mean that sex, train travel, or experiences near death do not exist.

When I get on a plane to fly to the United States, I expect to meet Americans when I arrive. My expectations are nearly always fulfilled when I arrive at the customs desk. Does this mean I am deluded or that my expectations have created U.S. customs officials?

There is also the inverse problem of all the people who expect to see things but never do. If only expectations were that powerful. All the afterlife expecters could live on forever, all the materialists could die and stay dead, and wealth and poverty could be reduced not to the exercise of human will and opportunity but merely the existence of hope. What a world that would be. But that is not how the world works, and expectations are simply not that decisive in their worldly effects.

In this book so far, I have argued that current research about hallucinations is not equipped in epidemiological or neurological terms to determine that these are freak anomalies. They do not appear to be. On the other hand, I do not have the evidence to connect these encounters to the history of mystical theology.

But I encourage you not to be a ping-pong ball in the tiresome debate about whether these experiences are "real." They are as real as anything that is considered real, and furthermore, they are commonplace. They are not abnormal. And from here we can explore something just as precious, something beyond the either-or debates common to this area. And that is the question of why these beings come to us and what they want. Whether from outside ourselves or inside ourselves, knowing why and what can help us. Our memories of the past are both inside and outside ourselves, they happened and did not happen, they are a mixture of "fact" and "interpretation." Personal experience approaches these definitions but is never identical with them. That is what these visitors are: part inside us, part outside us, part fact, part interpretation, and more than the sum of these parts. A tree that speaks to us. What does it say?

The Speaking Tree

When I started researching these experiences back in the 1990s, I was struck by one simple fact: the repetitious pattern of experience at their core. Some fifty years after the publication of Raymond Moody's best seller *Life after Life*, the internet is replete with first-person accounts. There are thousands of accounts of mystical experiences and just as many on booksellers' shelves. You need only read one or two books to get the gist.

They talk about out-of-body experiences, being drawn through a form of darkness (sometimes tunnel-like), meeting a bright being of light, experiencing some kind of life review without judgment, and meeting deceased friends, relatives, even pets. Some people report extraordinary environments with new colors, indescribable music, pastoral scenes, and sometimes cityscapes. The personal sense is one of unconditional love and acceptance, of coming home.

Deathbed and bereavement visions are less dramatic. In these visions, it is common to see dead friends and relatives. Many of these visits are full-bodied visions, meaning that the dying or the bereaved see the outline of their dead. Conversations are had, sometimes at great length. At other times, the dying or the bereaved sense only a "presence" or hear a voice. The books or the internet clips begin a narrative that is either frankly religious (Jesus is alive and well and we met and exchanged business cards) or rather more vague and "spiritual" (there is no death, fear not, this world is just the beginning of a roller coaster ride that will blow your mind). What is wrong with these pictures?

For me, as a social science researcher, these are like episodes of *The Twilight Zone*. Here you are walking along in life, minding your own business, then, all of a sudden, out of nowhere, Rod Serling appears on the sidewalk in front of you and tells you how your life and everything you understood are about to be turned upside down. None of the usual courtesies apply. There seems to be no reason why Rod has shown up. He seems not to be interested in you precisely but rather just ushers you into your newest shock series of events. There appears to be no continuity to this incident—he appears as though out of a jack-in-the-box. The NDE narrative is often literally narrated this way. But this is not what happens. Dying takes time, even when it seems sudden to onlookers.

Bereavement, like dying, is a process that unfolds. In both dying and bereavement, the scene, so to speak, must be set. The appearances are rarely (not never, but rarely) from strangers. Appearances, no matter how unusual, are part of the dying or bereaved person's web of relationships. No one barges into your life when you are dying or grieving. The visits follow a protocol like the rest of life's relationships. The dead follow rules. And I am not just being British

Perception

here. I am being anthropological. Living creatures reflect customs so that relationships and relationship encounters make sense.

In the coming chapters, I will describe the key features of the greetings and solicitations of these encounters. It is these forms of social life that give these encounters their fundamental meaning to those who are embraced by them. Descriptions of just these kinds of social customs, rationales, and rules demonstrate the normality of these interactions and underline that these are not abnormal aspects of our psychology. They are not to be grouped with the nightmares and hallucinations that are so often identified with serious mental illness or organic brain syndromes.

These kinds of encounters and experiences near death demonstrate all the social and cultural characteristics of our other social relationships because they are extensions of them. They are merely further evidence of our own idiosyncratic relationships, our biased but biographically determined perceptions, and our particular interpersonal and social needs. In other words, the work of our usual and normal relationships in everyday life, but this time at the end of life. As Victor Frankl's death camp patient expressed it, these experiences are our own speaking tree.

PART II

Patterns of Custom and Solicitation

4

Greetings and Other Customs

THERE ARE THOUSANDS upon thousands of stories about the dead visiting their living. The one I chose to share here is from an English woman I met called Sally. Her story[1] has all the essential characteristics of an encounter from the recently dead that are important to note for any future discussion.[2]

> My Nan was always fantastic to me and I have always loved her to bits. She and I had come from something of a dysfunctional family but the two of us had always managed to have a good relationship. She had been through quite a bit. Our family was dispersed all over the place because of the First World War. Nan became a bride in the Second World War and had three babies during that war, and then later another one. She was widowed fifteen years after World War Two just when the youngest was a teenager. After that time, a steady stream of family immigrated bit by bit to Australia from England. Eventually, my family was all the family that Nan had.

Many years ago she began to experience dementia. It was not recognized 'til quite late because Nan was good at hiding it. She worked hard and holidayed glamorously with her single friends (almost to the very end she dressed like Ingrid Bergman in the film *Casablanca*). She retired early, in 1981, and seemed to grow inwards from that time. Eventually she ended up in a nursing home with only me visiting her (the dysfunctional family endures!). She died in January 2012.

At the time of her death I had a lot going on, including considerable family fallout and trying to raise a five-year-old daughter as a single mum. Then a funny thing happened, and, as I mentioned, a lot was going on in my life then. One night, a month or two after Nan died, not long after I had gone to bed, I was just settling into bed, tucked up to my chin, half conscious in the pitch black. And then all of sudden—and I swear this, I am not religious—I felt a freezing gust of breeze against my left cheek followed almost immediately by a warm, loving kiss.

I am convinced my Nan, my dear old Nan, bless her . . . I am convinced she kissed me. Nothing like that had ever happened to me before, and certainly has not happened since. It gave me the most wonderful feeling, which has stayed with me. I was going through a lot of trouble at the time, and it was like her kiss made me feel warm, and loved—and maybe not protected—but strong!

I want to single out four important social facts about this story.

First, the encounter begins with a greeting, the kiss.

Second, this is a story about encouragement. The visit provides Sally with a new direction. Dead Nan's simple act encourages, supports, even directs Sally to be strong.

Third, there is, in this simple and seemingly pastoral act, not only encouragement but, through the renewal of the relationship, a reorientation, even transformation. Sally moves from a sense of being beleaguered and in trouble to a sense of strength and renewal. She finds a new sense of power, one that has stayed with her.

And finally, the person at the center of this story feels she has been given a gift through this encounter.

But in this chapter we will discuss the first of these features—the greeting.

Greeting Rites

Greetings have been described by anthropologists from all over the world as an almost universal human custom. People greet each other. This act is the first step in threat reduction. People who individually walk or run up to others without so much as a greeting to demonstrate their friendliness or identity are commonly perceived to be potentially dangerous. A greeting does not require a lot of content, just enough to indicate you mean no harm—a wave of the hand, a brief show of identity, the extension of a handshake, and so on.

There are many ways to greet—opening a door, answering the phone, saying hello, unlatching a gate, or in the above case, a kiss—that are common among the living as well as the dead. For the anthropologist Raymond Firth, greetings are always attention-producing, demanding recognition, and crucial to the reduction of uncertainty.[3] In Sally's story, Nan greets her with a kiss, recognized to be from her, and in that act identifies herself to Sally, who otherwise might have looked for competitive explanations—faulty room air-conditioning, a deranged burglar, sudden facial neurasthenia, and so on.

Many greetings are described as *phatic*, meaning that they set the tone for communication and have little real content in themselves. The anthropologist Esther Goody exemplified and categorized spoken greetings that refer to the time of day ("Good morning"), those that refer to activities ("Going for a walk, are we?"), those that refer to the weather ("Nice day!"), those that refer to health ("How are you?"), and those that refer to special times ("Merry

Christmas!").[4] It is not the content but rather the message behind the actual greeting that is most important. This says: I wish you well, I wish you no harm, let me reassure you, let me put you at ease. Greetings are an unsolicited gift. According to the linguist Guy Aston, they are necessary but not totally beholden to further, more important transactions and exchanges.[5]

In a study of front-door rituals between friends, the language scholars Christine Beal and Veronique Traverso noted five physical steps of greeting.[6] First, there is a knock on the door or a ringing of the bell. Then the door is opened. There are preliminary exchanges, like handshakes or verbal greetings. Then the guests move to the living room. Here they sit or make themselves at home.

This is the same pattern of interaction between family and friends who know each other but where one of them is dead. Sally's case, for example, begins with an alert, like a knock on the door: a brush of freezing air on her cheek. Her attention has been gained or oriented (the opening of the door), and a kiss, which is the actual greeting, is then placed on the cheek. Moving to the living area of the host can be interpreted as the visitor moving into our space as the new feelings begin to emerge within one's self—the personal or private space where we are. In Sally's case, there is also the physical fact that her Nan has come into Sally's bedroom for this visit. After the physical greeting of the kiss comes the recognition that this is her Nan, and Sally confesses to feeling "warm and loved." In other words, Sally "gets" comfortable with her visitor, but then her visitor leaves. It turns out that Nan has just popped by to drop off a gift of encouragement.

Greetings from bereavement visions have been documented to come through the telephone, by hand touch, from shaking a leg, by speaking the name of the bereaved to wake them from sleep, or by simply saying hi.[7] But it is important to note, despite the anthropologists' adamancy about the cross-cultural importance of greetings between humans, we do not, in fact, always use greetings. Furthermore, all those who visit us may not be human—at least not as we are accustomed to thinking about typical humans. For the moment, let's just talk about the human customs.

Continuance Customs

When I move from one room to another—at work or at home—I do not greet or regret those in my own home or at my immediate workplace. In other words, greetings do not apply to all human meetings all the time. Usually, some time must pass before we greet each other again. When I am at home, everyone usually knows I am there even if no one has seen me for some hours. I know I have not gone anywhere, and therefore I feel no need to greet anyone I have already greeted. On the odd occasion when I have walked into a room at work or at home and surprised someone in that room, they greet me with, "Oh, I thought you'd gone to the timetabling meeting" or "I thought you'd left to go to work." However, if we are both home and running into each other, we do not keep greeting each other. We simply begin an exchange—as the saying goes—picking up where we left off, if not in terms of actual conversation flow then in taken-for-granted relationship rapport and continuation. It is the same with interactions with the dead.

Consider the following two examples. In the first, Sonia speaks about the aftermath of the death of her nine-year-old daughter Valerie. Valerie died suddenly of a brain hemorrhage. On an evening about six weeks after Valerie's death, Sonia recounts,

> I went to bed quite early because I had exhausted myself, but I know I was awake. I was lying on my right side, and I felt someone touch my shoulder. I turned over and Valerie was standing there! She seemed real to me. She looked exactly like herself and in good health. She was bright, sort of glowing, and was dressed in a sparkling, dazzling white gown. She said, "Mommy, I love you. My headache is gone. I'm all right, and I don't want you to

Patterns of Custom and Solicitation

worry about me." She was very calm and happy and quite beautiful. Then, suddenly, she was gone.[8]

In the second example, Ken Ring, the psychologist and early near-death studies researcher, describes a woman's account of meeting her deceased parents during her own brush with death. I quote first that part of the account that describes the initial contact with her deceased mother:

> Then suddenly I saw my mother, who had died about nine years ago. And she was sitting—she always used to sit in her rocker, you know—she was smiling and she just sat there looking at me and she said to me in Hungarian [the language her mother had used while alive], "Well. We've been waiting for you. We've been expecting you. Your father's here and we're going to help you."[9]

In recalling the meeting with her father, she describes no greeting of any sort but rather a simple but meaningful question, "Did you bring your violin?" Just so, in Sonia's story, the nine-year-old deceased Valerie launches into an affirmation of her love for her mother, immediately reassuring her. Valerie was clearly in a hurry. Short message for a short visit. This is similar to Sally's Nan, whose brief message was one of support and encouragement. And although Sally's message was opened by a greeting (the kiss), the other messages in themselves are not greetings.

What are the most basic initial observations we can make about these rather typical accounts of first contact? First, in these latter accounts there is no formal greeting of the kind we see in Sally's earlier account. There is no verbal greeting, no handshakes, no kiss on the cheek, no "Hi there!" Just, "Did you bring your violin?" or "We've been waiting."

In all these cases, including Sally's, there is warmth and there is intimacy. However, it seems that formal greetings are dispensed with. The key to understanding this slip of convention may be that greetings are more important if the person at the center of the experience is asleep, about to sleep, or distracted. This might mean that the deceased visitor must seize the living person's attention in a more formal way (a knock at the door) and then identify themselves (through physical or verbal greeting). When the contact is fully visual and between intimates of long standing, like parents or lovers or children, the identity is obvious and formalities are bypassed.

Second, if social conventions in everyday life are any guide to the social conventions of dead people, then it may well be that the dead feel they have not gone anywhere. In other words, they—like me in my examples of being at home with my family—may feel that they have not lost contact. On realizing that we (the living) suddenly see them (the dead), they are likely to feel they can pick up where they left off.

This may be why Valerie mentions that she no longer has a headache six weeks after she had one. This may have been the last conversation she had with her mother, and so this is where she starts. The surprise, if a surprise is to be had, will be from the living not having seen the dead for some days, weeks, or even years. However, that may not be the dead person's experience. They may act as if they have been in touch the whole time, as in my example of working in another room all day. It is you who will act surprised, not me. I know where I have been.

Finally, the expression of greetings or continuance may have less to do with, or may be less moderated by, considerations of social convention than the practicalities of the medium. There seems to be no rhyme or reason as to why some contact with the deceased lasts a few seconds and some lasts a few minutes, or why some of the dead make full-blown audio-visual appearances and others only visual or only audio. Whether you believe the visits are a function of the mind or of the afterlife, we do not know why visits by the dead are brief or long, or why the appearances have so much variation. But if anyone has any idea about these matters, it might be expected that the dead might. And if that is the case, the practicalities of a kiss on the cheek versus a full-blown audio-visual appearance for the dead might be quite complex. If you were offered five seconds to say hello, how would you do it? Would you send a photo or a text message, or perhaps place a kiss on someone's cheek? Whatever the practicalities, if there are any practicalities, this influence must not be discounted in the evaluation of the significance of greeting and continuance from the visiting dead.

AS WE KNOW, the dead are not the only regular visitors to the living in near-death experiences (NDEs), deathbed visions (DBVs), or visions of the bereaved (VBs). There are also beings of light. The most common and famous beings of light are those found in accounts of NDEs from illness or an accident. These people commonly report out-of-body experiences, sensations of flying through dark spaces, a tunnel-like experience, and then breaking through into a world of light. The image of light is a surprisingly complex one, and many casual observers and writers commonly confuse this multiplicity of light phenomena.

Early near-death studies researchers distinguished four types of light phenomena: beings of light previously unknown to the experiencer, cities of light, brightly lit environments of light, and beings of light who may or may not be recognized as formerly known human beings.[10] To complicate matters further, Raymond Moody and Paul Perry identify "senior" beings of light:

> After meeting several beings of light, the NDEr usually meets a supreme Being of Light. People with a Christian background often describe him as God or Jesus. Those with other religious backgrounds may call him Buddha or Allah. But some have said that's its neither God nor Jesus, but someone very holy nonetheless. Whoever it is, the Being radiates total love and understanding.[11]

In the matter of greetings and continuance, consider the following two cases of visitations. First, the physician Melvin Morse recounts the NDE of a fourteen-year-old boy. During a cardiac arrest, in which the boy was obviously unconscious, the boy watched resuscitation efforts upon him while out of his own body. As he watched, he suddenly became aware of two beings of light that silently took up positions on either side of him. He recalls that these beings "gave him a sense of peace, love, and understanding."[12] They asked him whether he would like to go with them or stay on earth. He opted to stay.

In the second account, the journalist Katherine Russell Rich writes about the time when she was diagnosed with breast cancer at age thirty-two. You will remember Katherine's story from the opening chapter of this book, where she describes a moment of despair that was interrupted by the presence of an unusual light. Let us reconsider her account, taking particular note of exactly how the light enters her life and how Katherine reacts.

> In November, a curious thing happened. On the night before my thirty-third birthday, I was lying in bed, face to the wall, crying. Despondence had burned off the Scotch I'd drunk, and was now propelling me into hysteria. Between sobs, I'd go rigid, and it was in one of those moments of silence that I sensed a presence in the room behind me. Startled, I turned my head and saw a diffuse violet light shining through the bedroom door. The light didn't scare me, it soothed me, in fact, and within seconds, I was calm. Puzzled by this sudden well-being—the tears weren't even dry—I tried to work myself back into hysteria, but couldn't. My anguish had vanished, drained by the light. A sense of security overtook me, the first I felt in years, and soon I was asleep.... Ten years on, the memory remains indelible, still potent and still inexplicable.[13]

Note in both of these cases, the beings of light arrive unannounced and offer no greetings whatsoever. Though without social graces, they are nevertheless not without any redeeming features. Neither the boy nor Katherine perceives the lights to be threatening. Nor do they seem to insert more uncertainty or terror into the situation when they inexplicably appear. For my own part, if a being of light appeared in my lounge (whether or not I had a single malt scotch), I would be unsettled to say the least. And yet, a young boy and an educated young journalist receive these visitors with apparent equanimity.

We see here an absence of greeting and an absence of continuance. What accounts for the behavior of this new and novel social intrusion? Why are these two not shocked by what is not only a strange being by any criteria but also one that appears as unannounced as a burglar?

Because many of these beings of light are strangers, they should, according to most customs, greet us. But once again we must look to the different social conventions around meetings. Mostly friends, family, and coworkers greet each other when they meet after a time, even a short time. The greetings are always informal. Kisses are not out of place, at least in Europe. Even these informal greetings can be dispensed with if the period of separation is short or there is no acknowledged real separation—such as having been just over in the next room. This is called *continuance*.

But aside from greetings and continuance, there are circumstances that merit neither social custom. Think of when you have been waiting at a bus stop or train platform and people begin to complain to each other about the delay. Or think about a crisis, where you are all huddled together avoiding some violence on the street or grabbing hold of the same fixtures during an earthquake. People start to talk, without introduction and with continuance, even though they are strangers to each other. Why?

Because in distress, company is welcome. Formal greetings are unnecessary because, for all intents and purposes, the individuals are already acquainted. They are in it together. They are covictims, cohabitants, participants in the same scene. Sometimes, in these situations, people will offer each other bits of food or candy or chewing gum, perhaps a cigarette. Introductions may soon follow if the circumstances persist.

Mostly, the beings of light seem to appear in times of crisis. Katherine receives an important visit during her despair over her cancer diagnosis. The boy is an onlooker to his own emergency resuscitation. The beings of light look on—they are co-experiencers by any criterion. They are engaged in and with what happens, and they share the experience with their new human company. But there is more.

Imagine getting a flat tire when you are driving in a strange place on a rainy night. All you want to do is get home, to where things are normal and usual for you. Out of the dark, a stranger approaches with a wheel jack, tire iron, and lug wrench and offers to help. He may or may not greet you. He simply acknowledges your predicament and offers to help. But wait, there is more still.

Strangers do not necessarily need to greet you or introduce themselves when they are wearing, for example, a police uniform, a cleric's habit, or a paramedic's uniform. In these cases, greetings are optional because you *know* who they are and why they are there. They are there to help. The uniform is the continuance of a larger, more abstract relationship. They are first responders or part of a wider social institution of social care and welfare. We recognize them immediately.

How do we recognize that beings of light are in this institutional category? For one, they wear a uniform. They are bathed in a warm and welcoming light. And there is no ambiguity to their presence. Like the stranger with the tire iron, the beings bring with them emotional tools to help, and these are instantaneous. They bring peace, reassurance, knowledge, help, support, and calm. That is why, I imagine, neither the boy nor Katherine was alarmed. Both their appearance and their service behavior suggest that, although not friend or family, they are not, strictly speaking, strangers. They are recognizable service personnel who are there to help—police in a break-in, firemen at a smoking house, an emergency plumber at a blocked drain about to flood your home.

In this cultural way, beings of light are examples of continuance. While we often think of continuance as the smooth, informal social relations of known friends and family, and greetings as the proper rituals that govern new interactions and reimmersion into old ones, it is also the case that reimmersion rituals govern our understanding of social service interactions. The service and the uniform are the greeting. And they bring the help we need, as opposed to the help we want from family and friends.

The most important and most interesting anthropological fact about customs of continuance is that all parties have a mutual understanding of the beneficence of the relationships involved. As the term *continuance* implies, there is a constancy to the relationship, and that is somewhat surprising since most visitors are dead, and most survivors believe that they will never see them again. And some visitors, like the beings of light, are new arrivals for most who report them. Yet the service and appearance they convey send out an old and reassuring message. Because that kind of help is not unprecedented, it is neither novel, nor unsettling, nor threatening. This message is also infused into our emotional state so that we know instantly this is help and not threat. How the beings of light do this I do not know, but it is apparent from first-person accounts that this is their effect, and affect, on their charges. Greetings and customs of continuance are therefore hallmark features of the initial contact of encounters near death both of those whom we know (our dead) and those we do not know (our beings of light).

A Taxonomy of Greeting Customs

From the above review of how these near-death visitors introduce themselves we can deduce a strong pattern of social customs familiar in our own everyday life. Deceased relatives and friends follow the social rules of their origins—our world. Beings of light, although unprecedented in our everyday world, also follow behaviors that we recognize and for which we find precedence in our own lives. By careful description of how they seem to behave, we may identify their social functions and locate them within similarly performing social groups in our own society. The way even these unusual beings relate tends to follow the customary behavior we are used to in other familiar human group interactions.

Overall, then, we can identify two important groups and their customary greetings: the Familiars (our dead whom we know) and a group we might call the Emergency Social Services. Familiars can offer both formal and informal greetings. In formalized greetings, familiars attempt to rouse or alert us to their presence when we are preoccupied—for example, asleep. These are literally attention-producing greetings in the classic anthropological sense. A parallel function of this formal greeting is that sometimes this style of greeting can itself be the message. Commonly, as in Sally's case, that message is a simple theme of reassurance: "I'm OK, and so are you."

In the more informal greeting type—what I have termed a *continuance style contact*—the greeting is an underlying function. By *underlying function* I mean to suggest that identity recognition is immediate and the renewal of a train of conversation or thought between two people who know each other is an explicit sign of reacquaintance. It is, for all intents and purposes, a greeting, albeit an implicit one, between familiars. However, unlike formal greetings it is the message of the contact that is privileged. Themes for these kinds of continuances seem to be the following: "Where were we? Ah, yes, do you remember . . ." or "I'm not going anywhere; I'm just next door" or "I need you to know or do something for me or for yourself." Similar to formal greetings, this kind of continuance greeting provides important reassurance and reaffirmation. Occasionally, a request may be made of the dying person or the bereaved.

DEAD FAMILIARS

Formal Greetings
Attention producing

Main Theme
"I'm OK, you're OK"

Informal Greetings
Continuance/implicit/informal

Main Themes
"Where were we? Ah, yes . . ."
"I'm nearby"
"I need you to know/do"

Finally, in a second type of continuance greeting, beings of light behave like emergency workers—but in this case, emergency social service workers. They commonly appear in crisis situations, often suddenly and unannounced, but their appearance and communications, such as they are, are immediately and unambiguously reassuring. Their messages seem to be the following: "You're not alone," "How can we help?," "At your service," and "You have a choice here that we can help with; what would you like to do?"

BEINGS OF LIGHT

Informal Greetings
Continuance/institutional

Main Theme
"You're not alone"
"How can we help?"
"At your service"
"You have a choice here, and we can help"

Do the Dead Bid Farewell?

At the end of the visit, do the dead or the beings of light formally sign off? In this chapter I have shown several typical examples of interactions with the dead and beings of light. Sally and her brief encounter with her kissing Nan. Sonia's account of a visit from her dead daughter Valerie. Ken Ring's NDE interviewee who meets her mother and father, who ask whether she brought her violin. A fourteen-year-old boy who meets two beings of light while watching himself be resuscitated. And Katherine Russell Rich's violet being of light behind her bedroom door. In none of these examples do the visitors say goodbye or ask to take their leave. They simply leave or, worse, simply disappear without a word.

Early in my career I studied the farewell behavior of a hundred people dying of cancer.[14] All of the respondents in my study had quite specific plans for how they would leave friends and family. The overwhelming majority (some 80 percent) had plans or had already instituted plans to say their farewells before their own death. The reasons for this conduct were entirely understandable—they were leaving, and they did not want to leave without saying goodbye. Kudos to them for following expected convention, because it is not only they who want to bid farewell; most of their family and friends want the chance to say goodbye to their dying loved one.

The social functions of such conduct also make sense in the culture of everyday ritual. The giving and receiving of farewells signals to all parties that each of them is worthy of a last goodbye.[15] Like most greetings in general, all farewells in this context are gifts. Farewells reaffirm the perceived value of past and present relationships, ensuring a place in the memory for future ones.

Farewells make the physical departures "real" by creating them as social acts beforehand.[16] In this way, farewells as social conduct prepare and mirror physical departures, softening and graduating any departure. Farewells grease the cogs of interaction, making them predictable and allowing us to feel in control. They also warn others of future inaccessibility.[17] They create a sense of finality and closure that permits all actors to switch their attention from the priorities of now to the priorities of the next. In the context of dying, this allows survivors to prepare for grief, and the dying person to prepare for what is to come, whatever that may be. Since most people in the context of dying think they will soon never see each other again, certainly in this life, farewells are crucially important for the dying and those around them. But what if you are already dead? Does it make any social sense to say goodbye?

Nearly 20 percent of my respondents in that early study refused to bid farewell. It may well be here, in this subsample, that we might understand why someone would not want to say goodbye in the context of dying. Those I interviewed gave one of four answers when I asked them why they would not bid farewell. The first was that farewells make endings too intense and upsetting. Others said it was only a temporary separation anyhow. Some had made farewells earlier and saw no point in making them again. And some wanted to keep things "normal," and felt that farewells could be emotionally and socially disruptive.

For people experiencing DBVs, it makes no sense that their dead companions would say goodbye, because they are actually in the process of welcoming them. They are saying hello. For the bereaved who are visited by their dead, there can be no doubt that these are emotionally charged reunions. Whether it is my old piano teacher, who was visited by her dead mother, or Sonia, who was visited by her dead daughter, one must ask an important question here: Do the dead want to inject more emotion into the temporary reunion than they already have? The event is clearly designed to give advice or provide a new direction or insight for the person they have visited. Most people are already very surprised anyway. Almost all recipients are grieving. Except for those for whom the visit is a chance to say goodbye, saying goodbye again may only reopen the wound. This reason is consistent with the first and third reasons why many dying people avoid farewells—avoiding the upset and revisiting what has already taken place.

The second reason, which is minor for dying people but may be a major reason for the dead and their light friends, is that they all believe that the separation is only temporary anyway—as their visit plainly evidences—and it is a mere artifice to go through social conventions of endings when this is not how the dead or beings of light actually experience the relationship.

This brings us to the final reason offered by dying people for not bidding farewells. Dead people want things to appear "normal"—their acts and messages, and their emotional infusions into the inner life of the survivors are designed to signal continuance, not endings. They might not want to direct their loved ones to think of their relationships as over—quite the opposite, it seems—they want their loved ones to know that they continue to play a role in their everyday lives in one way or another, more or less.

So while most dying people want to say goodbye, those among the dead who make it back for postmortem contact want to give the opposite impression. This may be one reason why the largest book on cases of VBs is entitled *Hello from Heaven*. Although we do not know what heaven is, or whether any of our dead come from there, we can certainly acknowledge that most of the efforts of the dead who visit us—in altered states of consciousness near death, in our bereavement, or on our deathbed—are busy putting their efforts into one main greeting: "Hello again."

5
Advice

THE BOOK OF ACTS tells the story of Saul of Tarsus.[1] Although most people read this as a famous conversion story about a man who became the apostle Paul, we will consider how his incident illustrates a confrontation with a being of light in whom he did not believe. You will not be surprised if I say that, a couple of thousand years later notwithstanding, this heavy-handed style of attention seeking from the world of the invisible remains an all-too-common story. Saul's story reminds us of two lessons about mystical beings and the dead: they do not like to be forgotten, and they forcefully advise and direct us.

Saul was a Jewish Pharisee and a member of the Roman mafia who killed or facilitated the killing of early Christians. He did it well, he did it often, and he was workmanlike at it. On one particular day, on his commute from his office to his next appointment in Damascus, he is suddenly knocked to the ground by a large, all-encompassing flash of light.

Depending on the translation of the witness reports, it was either a lightning strike or an inexplicable blast of light from nowhere.

Saul ends up spread-eagle on the road as a booming voice, emanating from the light, rings in his ears. The voice within the light asks Saul why he is persecuting him.[2] Saul, still unable to see the person addressing him because of the aftereffects of the light on his eyes, denies all culpability. As with many offenders caught red-handed, Saul's denial buys time.

The voice from the light instructs Saul to go into Damascus and wait for a caller. By the time he arrives in town, he realizes that he has not recovered from the flash of light and is now blind. While he waits, he is visited by a Christian named Ananias, who restores his sight. Saul becomes Paul, and the rest is Christian history. Paul became one of Christianity's greatest missionaries.

For our purposes, the lesson from the story is that not all beings of light merely keep company, and not all are particularly friendly. However, if this story is anything to go by, even the pushy beings of light, like the one described here, initiate a review of life that makes their recipients rethink their current direction. This rethink of biographical purpose, values, or current experience is a theme in visits from our dead too.

In the previous chapter I described Sally's experience of a visit from her dead Nan. In that story Nan comes to Sally as she is settling into bed, just about to fall asleep. Sally experiences a breeze against her cheek followed by a warm kiss. She is convinced that this kiss is from Nan. Note here Sally's exact words: "Her kiss made me feel warm, and loved—and maybe not protected—but strong!" Sally was noticing how the interaction had agency; in other words, it had a directing effect on her feelings toward some emotional sensations (e.g., support and confidence) and away from others (e.g., worry and troubled). Like Saul and his encounter with a being of light, Sally did not have a simple sociable but passive encounter but rather one that had a strong purpose and action.

Some visions of the bereaved (VBs) are more specific in their directives, offering, as they did in Saul's encounter, direct advice. In 2014, the UK-based newspaper *The Guardian* reported the unusual story of an Iranian execution that was halted.[3] A man named Balal was about to face public execution by hanging for his crime of murder in Iran. As a teenager, seven years earlier, Balal was involved in a street fight with another teenager in a local marketplace. Balal pulled a knife and stabbed the other boy to death. Now he stood on a chair, on a public gallows, blindfolded, with a noose around his neck. Iran has more executions than almost all countries except China. According to Sharia law, the victim's family, who were present on the day of the execution, were permitted to participate in Balal's execution by pushing the chair on which he stood.

The journalist Saeed Kamali Dehghan describes what happened next: "The victim's mother approached, slapped the convict in the face, and then decided to forgive her son's killer. The victim's father removed the noose and Balal's life was spared."[4]

Asked why they had spared their son's killer, the father replied, "Three days ago my wife saw my elder son in a dream, telling her that they are in a good place, and for her not to retaliate. . . . This calmed my wife and we decided to think more until the day of the execution."

Personal dreams, such as this one from Iran, have always been important to the religious life of Islamic societies. They are commonly viewed as sources of revelation about the mysteries of this world and the next.[5]

This chapter explores how advice and purposeful direction are long-standing customs of the visiting dead. These customs are part of a broader culture of how the dead have been viewed as troublesome, meddlesome, or just plain helpful. They are also a key reason many cultures develop ways to ward them off, or at least attempt to constrain them by religious habit and ritual. In our contemporary and more secular society, the old customs have fallen away, but the visits still come. When customs are forgotten, the reasons for them are often forgotten too. Here we will restore some of these anthropological insights.

Advice

Meddling and Pedaling

In 1911 and 1912, the anthropologist Sir James Frazer delivered a series of lectures at St. Andrews University in Scotland that would become the basis of his three-volume treatise *The Belief in Immortality and the Worship of the Dead*.[6] This was a transcultural review of beliefs about the dead and their fate among the peoples of the Pacific. Frazer repeatedly described the many ways that the dead participate in the lives of the living. Variations to these beliefs aside for a moment, the major findings are that a number of the dead continue to live among the living for a short time after death, some for months, and some, occasionally, for years. This group usually does so for a reason, and if the reason is addressed, they stop visiting. It is a simple set of ideas, but trouble follows when it is forgotten.

Frazer reminds us that most cultures recognize the dead as people who gradually withdraw from life. The dead are not alive one minute and suddenly dead the next, even though that is our current stereotype. In traditional cultures, the dead must be listened to and appeased so that they can move on to wherever they are going—a hole in the earth, another island, or a place in the sky. The final destination does not much matter. What matters is ensuring that whatever they need, they get. Often this need is simple—recognition and respect—and once it is fulfilled, off they go. However, if the rites have not been performed or have been performed poorly, or if they have a personal issue with someone, the dead will linger. Throughout human history our dead and their associates have come either in dreams (as for the Iranian mother) or in waking hours (as for Saul and Sally).

The dead are often described by traditional cultures as mischievous, touchy, and admonishing but also as informing and consoling. All come with advice or directives for the living. Many cultures fear these visits and try to prevent them by ensuring that the dead have everything they need in their grave goods or their burnt offerings. Other people show their respect by performing signs of grief, like self-cutting in the immediate period after death. Still others are more aggressive in their commitment to stop the dead from returning—decapitating them, puncturing their lungs, or staking them through the heart. These customs are not confined to the traditional cultures of the Pacific but have parallels in medieval and ancient European cultures too, in one context or another. Throughout human history, the dead have been expected to return if nothing is done to stop them.

The historian R. C. Finucane reminds us of the culture-specific nature of many of these visits and the structure and purpose of the stories told about them. In medieval Christian times, stories about visits from the dead were told to justify the church's teaching on morality, to assure believers of the afterlife, or to remedy some injustice in the social realm.[7] Finucane argues that as the culture-specific nature of the expectations change, so do the characteristics and purpose of the visits from the dead.[8]

There is truth in Finucane's insights insofar as he confines himself to "ghost" sightings or sightings of the dead as seen through the eyes of oracles, soothsayers, saints, holy monks, and modern mediums. But for the close-up and rather more pedestrian encounters between ordinary men and women who are near death or surviving the death of someone they loved, the customs and messages have remained remarkably consistent, stable, and personal. Our intimate dead and beings of light have *not*, in the main, sung from the cultural scripts of the day's religion or politics.

However, what all of these public or private accounts have in common is purpose: they are there to provide direction.

In people who have had near-death experiences (NDEs), reports abound of beings of light or the dead advising the dying person to stop, go back, that it is not "their time." Even Frazer's 1913 review of nineteenth-century Pacific accounts contains similar stories. Among the Hervey Islanders, it was a common belief that souls who were not meant to be dead would be told by some kindly spirits

Advice

that they must "go back and live."[9] This injunction by dead familiars is a common purpose in NDEs so that the living do not cut short what is their fair allotment in life.

In people who have deathbed visions (DBVs), the advice is often the opposite. The dead *wish* the dying to join them. Often when keeping their company, the dying will impatiently prompt the dying person to get on with it. Recall the cases in the opening chapter of the children who were urged by their dead grandmothers to join them as soon as possible. The advice is, "Let's go, spit-spot, don't be tardy, fun to be had here." And for the bereaved, the advice is often reassurance and encouragement to get on with the rest of their lives without the dead. As one correspondent recounts in his encounter with his former best friend, Scott, who had recently died of an acute infection: "I know I left this earth without settling (an) argument with you. I just wanted to tell you I'm sorry and that I love you very much. I'll be seeing you soon but not that soon." Reflecting on that message, Scott's friend recalls, "I woke up the next morning and felt a tremendous peace with him. I'll never forget this visit from him and will hold it in my heart until I pass from this earth and see him again."[10] The dead often claim to wait for us when our turn as living people is up. Their advice is usually to soldier on, be strong, have faith in yourself, be happy, be at peace.

In all these examples, the advice and the directives are not about which political party to vote for or which religion to join. The Iranian mother was not advised to oppose or support the death penalty in Iran. These ideological issues were irrelevant to her purposes and those of her dead. She was advised only to forgive. Traditional ghost "stories," as the phrase implies, are frequently designed for a public audience and public dissemination. Advice received while dying or bereaved, however, is mostly about personal growth and support, and the directives and purposes derived from it are often just as intimate. Advice and direction are always about reengagement in the lives of the living—meddling in the lives of the people with whom they were intimately connected and concerned, and pedaling advice the dead believe is crucial for the survivor's well-being.

Because customs for the dead are receding in modern industrialized societies, the formal sanctions to keep the dead at bay are also receding. The living do not expect the dead to bother them, because they do not believe they will. Overall belief in religion, the supernatural, and the afterlife is fading. For the dead, in theory anyway, this means far less cultural and personal messaging to stay away and move on and more opportunity to make emotional contact with their family and friends. The problem now, however, is that any such contact is far more likely to induce surprise in the recipient and later, difficulties in integrating that experience into a secular life without formal religions, or at least religions with little formal pareschatology.[11] While traditional cultures the world over had myths about what happens to the dead in the first few hours, days, and years, modern cultures and religions offer images of only the final resting places of souls, if any. The bereaved and the dying have little recent materials to draw on to explain their personal experiences. For many people lost in the wake of this secular wilderness, the recent literature on NDEs and VBs can guide them.

Why Advice?

There are at least three good reasons why the dead tend to offer advice and direction rather than information, counseling, or winning lottery numbers. Questions about the absence of these more ambitious requests or services have been raised by both conventional behavioral sciences and skeptical critics. But the anthropological answers make it fairly clear why the dead do not, in the main, offer these services. I say "in the main" here because there are claims by a few that the dead do occasionally give details of the afterlife. I am not here referring to those Dantean accounts that tell extensive travel stories about the afterlife (see, for example,

Advice

Eben Alexander's *Proof of Heaven* for one recent instance of what is clearly a genre with a long history in this field).[12]

Some who have had NDEs claim to have been given details of what the afterlife might look like. Some people on their deathbed have described parts of the afterlife they have been told about by their dead companion at their bedside. For example, they have been told that their dead friends and relatives await them, or that they will be able-bodied again soon. Some bereaved people have been given small details of the world in which their dead friend or relative now inhabits.

There are also countless cases where the bereaved or the dying were offered information about the whereabouts of an important document, or about the future health and welfare of a relative or friend.

Some years ago, a prominent member of the local chapter of skeptics asked to meet me over lunch to discuss my earlier book on the NDE. I happily agreed. Over coffee it gradually emerged that this hapless skeptic had an NDE himself quite recently. In it, he met a deceased friend who had been in the same professional field as himself. They discussed a few private matters, but during their exchange his dead friend shared a couple of important industrial formulas based on some currently unsolved technical problems.

After my skeptic friend recovered, he told no one about his experience for fear of ridicule. Furthermore, he published the formulas he had been shown in excellent peer-reviewed publications. As a skeptic, he was now unsure whether his previous beliefs that these NDEs were merely the misfiring neurons of a dying brain were relevant to what he had experienced. Furthermore, he could not explain away how real his experience had seemed to him, or how and why he received such important chemical information. He remained dismayed, though grateful, about the gift. But in all these exceptional instances, it should be noted that this is not the main reason for the contact, and the details are very brief and modest in description. Even my skeptical friend was provided only two formulas.

In the analysis of communications with one's dead, one must always bear in mind one crucial but practical question: How fit for purpose is advice or direction as a communication form compared with information giving, clairvoyance, or counseling?

Look at it this way. It does not take long to advise someone to stop, turn around, and go back, or to smile at someone, or to tell someone you love them. Describing a new world might take a bit longer. Describing more than one or two formulas might take longer still. Counseling someone about their current troubles might take much, much longer. So in other words, perhaps the first major reason why the dead and their associates give advice and direction is that these are economical. And NDEs, DBVs, and VBs are famously brief.

Most NDEs, certainly those in a resuscitation context, last only a few seconds. Minutes at most. Most of those near death are too ill to concentrate for long. Most VBs are brief. My old piano teacher saw her dead mother just long enough for her mouth to drop in surprise before her mother disappeared, as quickly as she arrived. In that time, she left a small smile and a lifetime impression.

So why not winning lottery numbers, then? Surely that would take only a few seconds. For this existentially important question, we would do well to recognize that the dead have not gone into the future (or they could not talk to us in the present), and they certainly have not gone into *our* future. Or it may simply be that since clairvoyants do not hand out winning numbers when they are alive, they probably perform even less optimally when dead. There are clearly limits to afterlife messaging services.

In the old anthropological literature, the dead who appear, even to strangers, never stay long. The anthropologist Bronislaw Malinowski, in one of his many treatises on the culture and customs of the people of the Trobriand Islands, tells a story about a party of men visiting a neighboring island known to be where the dead go after death.

Advice

They landed not far from the Modawasi stone, when they saw a man standing there. They immediately identified him as Go'iopeulo, a great warrior and a man of indomitable strength and courage, who had died recently in a village not more than five minutes' distance from Omarakana. When they approached, he disappeared, but they heard distinctly, "Bu Kusisusi bala" [you remain, I shall go], the usual form of good-bye. Another of my informants was in Tuma drinking water in one of the large water grottos, so typical of the raiboag (woods). He heard a girl called Buava'u Lagim cry out to him, calling him by name, out of this waterhole.[13]

In these old and non-Western case examples, we see again the brevity of the contact by the dead. They describe events that are seconds, not minutes, long. This is typical of the limits to dead communication among our familiars. Even in our earlier case of Saul or Katherine Russell Rich, the encounters last no more than a minute. Whatever lesson we take from these stories, the basic observation is one of brevity, and this alone must credibly be the most important factor in the shape and choice of any communication content.

The second important reason why the dead and their associates choose to dispense only advice and direction must be the marginal importance of information generally and afterlife information more specifically. The reasons for this are twofold. First, the information from the afterlife the dead may wish to convey is almost impossible to describe—that is, the world they now inhabit is ineffable or unknowable to us. We have some evidence that this might be the case. Second, the lack of information might simply reflect the actual unknown—the genuine absence of island or sky paradises, or the real lack of any eschatology of any substance. To put it another way, little is told because there is little to tell.

In Sir James Frazer's review of the Pacific people's view of the immortal life, nearly everyone has a clear idea of what the afterlife looks like. It looks like this life. The dead live on islands or caverns where they live in huts, fish, hunt, have sex, even reproduce, and fight with each other, just as they do in this life. Not much changes. There do appear to be some benefits: there is no scarcity of food, people seem happier, and either death is finally banished or reincarnation is ensured. Life goes on, connection with the world is mysteriously ongoing, although transforming.

There are some modern accounts of NDEs of people from these regions that suggest this type of continuity remains true of afterlife experiences for these people. In other words, the NDE accounts seem to mirror much of these beliefs in the material constancy of the afterlife infrastructures.[14] There are some unexpected anomalies too. Some huts float above the ground, seemingly unsupported by any structure, and people are certainly happier than traditional legends would seem to indicate. But the differences are small. In American and British accounts of NDEs, the picture of the afterlife is significantly different.

The ineffable nature of NDEs was reported almost from the very beginning by the first studies in this field. Raymond Moody,[15] Ken Ring,[16] and Carol Zaleski[17] are among the first modern researchers to discuss this problem of ineffability. Some two-thirds of people who had NDEs interviewed by Ken Ring could not describe the afterlife world they had visited.[18] They claimed to see unprecedented colors that were undescribable because the language for them was unavailable, or they described being given information that cannot be imparted either because they have no surviving memory of the details or because there was no way to express it in words.[19] As one of Ring's interviewees tells it: "Yeah, it was like—it was such—I've never had an experience like this. I mean, like, there's, like, no, no words—to convey it. Like when I was trying to tell you how the voice was and how the feeling [pause] of just drifting, you know, it was [pause] it was really weird. It's hard to explain in words."[20] On the other hand, Finucane may be right when he claims that messages from the dead reflect broader cultural expectations. Visions

Advice

from medieval Christians contained images, advice, or symbols from the afterlife world that support the expectations of the listener or percipient.[21] Visions from Victorian Spiritualists contained images, advice, or symbols that Spiritualists hold dear. And maybe, because in a secular society we hold no particular image sacred or have no clear idea of any afterlife, that is what comes across in our communications with the dead. Maybe those on their deathbed or in an NDE, because they have few preconceptions about the afterlife, are unsure *how* to describe what they are seeing, because they do not have the narrative wherewithal to describe it. They have no linguistic or mythical equipment, so to speak, to describe their observations. The emptiness or the vacuous nature of contemporary religious imagery of the afterlife is then reflected back to us by those equally without that equipment or by us in trying to reconvey that information to others. Maybe since both pareschatology and eschatology are no longer part of our cultural language, this is now reflected back to us in our encounters with the mysterious world of the "dead" and their colleagues.

The main problem with this last set of observations about the lack of a cultural script to employ to describe encounters with the dead is that many people who *do* have that equipment still find it unhelpful in describing their encounters. Nevertheless, if we play the devil's advocate momentarily, if there really is no afterlife, and the dead are some kind of hallucination for which we will one day have an adequate causal theory, then the absence of a real eschatological "place" will predict a type of information and communication content bereft of detail. This is possible, if not likely, given our other possibilities and experiences.

The third and final reason that advice and direction are the main style and content of communications from the dead is that the dead seem to be driven by *their* need to help, to support, to achieve, to redirect, to evidence, to resolve, or to gift. And the key to understanding that need is the universal experience of human attachment and loss. This experience of loss applies to grieving survivors of death as much as the grieving dead who still care about their separation from their loved ones.

Attachment and grief are the key reasons why the dead remain among us or return briefly to us, why they meddle, and why they pedal advice and directives. This is the main message in all the anthropological writings of the twentieth century. Today, we think about grief and bereavement as a clinical narrative about survivors. But in the past, traditional peoples also applied this theme of grief and loss to the social psychology of the dead, whatever later psychoanalytic or sociological theories were grafted on top of this ethnographic data by the materialist-secular likes of Sigmund Freud, Emile Durkheim, or Max Weber.[22] Modern social theory eventually eclipsed our own historical voices, obscured as they were by the post-Enlightenment rush to discredit or explain away their perceptions. Today, we remember the pop remnants of these traditions of analysis but forget the strength and prevalence of the original data these theories were designed to discredit.

Perhaps the most famous of all anthropological essays on the relationship of the living to the dead is Malinowski's essay "Death and the Reintegration of the Group."[23] In this essay, Malinowski describes how humanity has dual, ambivalent responses toward the dead. On the one hand, humanity cherishes the person who has died, wishes not to be parted from them, and clings to their memory and their material remains in the form of keepsakes and former possessions. On the other hand, these same bereaved people fear and are repulsed by the body corrupted by death. They fear the violence of bodily damage and decomposition. They fear the ghost or the wreck of bad luck, misfortune, or illness that death may bring in its wake. The bereaved wish to keep—and to reject. The bereaved mourn—but hide away. The bereaved know where the dead go, but they do not wish to follow.

The grieving survivors adorn themselves with paint, with dance, with ritual, with self-flagellations, and with the most public expressions of sorrow. They do this not only because they feel the pain of separation but also because they need to appease the dead and send them on their way. Everywhere we can see tendencies to preserve the remains *and* to be rid of them. Some cultures mummify or bury. Others cremate, cannibalize, or feed remains to predators. For some cultures, the dead are completely untouchable. Others must ritually eat some part of the corpse or smear the fat of the dead on their own skins. These practices illustrate the global ambivalence and tensions between love and attachment, on the one hand, and horror and abhorrence toward the dead, on the other. Malinowski argued that people are intensely afraid of death and, like the psychoanalytic touts before and after him, asserted that this required religion to harness this fear into a denial. That denial became the belief in spirits, "a result of the belief in immortality." The facts of animism itself lie "in the deepest emotional fact of human nature, the desire for life."[24]

This is a poetic academic narrative if only you overlook the non sequitur and conflations of the main grief objects of death. First, it is an ethnocentric insult to claim that early peoples could not tell the difference between dead bodies and their deceased personalities. Most people in most places understood the difference. Their belief in the continued existence of the dead usually insisted on a strict code of respect during the mortuary processes. Grief must be shown toward the deceased remains, but both the living and the dead know that these are remains, not zombies. Where beliefs *seem* to conflate these two subjects—the body and the personality—as when people decapitate or drive a stake into a body to prevent wandering, such acts suggest other beliefs. Either the personality associated with the body is reading off what is done to its former body as a way the living are communicating to them ("with respect, or with strident intent, please do go onto the afterlife world and leave us alone") or part of the dead spirit remains dependent on the body for power to act in this world. Any chance of reanimation, in the body or from the body as a source of (albeit fading) power, is addressed through mutilation of the remains. No one is suggesting that mutilation of a corpse is mutilation of the spirit. These acts are mostly communication acts from the living to the dead and occupy the same sociological and semiotic space as other mourning rituals.

Second, denial of death is one of the great self-serving explanations of the secular era. Short briefing here: Does personality survive death? We do not know. Most people believe it does. Many educated people believe it does not. The educated need an explanation to discredit those who believe in survival and to congratulate themselves on not being duped by the beliefs of the many. No one has any definitive evidence, but if they cannot see the basis for your evidence and that opposing side still believes, it is a safe bet to assert they are deniers.

Denial is an explanation you have when you do not have one. Clearly, people do not deny the reality of death, or else no one would hold a funeral. If seeing spirits is linked to beliefs in immortality, then those who see spirits but do not believe in immortality are in serious trouble. And as a matter of fact, many of them are in trouble. They struggle to come to grips with their own experience because they have no recourse to religious literacy or vocabulary. Denial is supposed to be a defense mechanism and operates temporarily in crisis. When it persists, it is called a belief. The evidence that denial persists in this precise psychodynamic way is modest to nonexistent, but if you resist that idea, well, you may yourself be in denial.

In the light of the historical and current facts about the prevalence of experiences near death, among those with widely diverse beliefs and those who do not believe, it is more likely that the experience of contact with the dead *preceded* the beliefs and, in fact, creates the need for these beliefs to warn and prepare others who have not had the experience. Even Malinowski remarked, "Religion saves man from a surrender to death and destruction, and in doing this it merely makes use of the observations of dreams, shadows, and visions."[25]

But the bottom line in all these deliberations about how we grieve for our losses is one principle: if any one of us does survive death, it should come as no surprise that we would wish to communicate with our former attachments. And that possibility, as the world's traditional cultures will attest, is one of the most powerful human drivers of all, alongside love itself. The dead return, if only for a moment, to assure those who love them of their well-being or to offer comfort or to return them to their own former path. These are all strong urges in anyone's grief, but for the dead there is only the briefest of moments in which to perform this cherished task. Advice and direction, then, are the dead's best bet for a surgically timed communication inside this fleeting of all opportunities—a last message. And a message that is culturally and psychologically understood by all persons who have experienced a significant loss, alive or dead.

6

Transformation

CAN A SINGLE INCIDENT change your life? Most people believe it can. A chance meeting with the person who will later become the love of your life. The birth of a child. Landing the job of your dreams. The diagnosis of a life-limiting illness. The death of a child.

These and many other incidents of this order could be understood as life changing, transforming, reorienting. But what about the simpler incidents in life? Could seeing a flower change your life? Could a dream change your life? Could a sense of a presence in your living room change your life?

Although most people will agree that undergoing one of life's great transitional rites of passage can change your life—birth, adulthood, marriage, graduation—it is a bit more difficult to see how the small things might do the same. Let me tell you about a small penny tucked away in the back pocket of my life. It is a story about a birthday and a fish and a lasting memory.[1]

When I turned twelve, I wanted to do something special for my birthday. After my parents separated, my mother and I were left poor by most standards. A trip away or a major gift was always out of the question. At the time, we were living in Sydney, Australia, quite near a major river. I decided I would go fishing to see if I could get lucky.

I got up at four in the morning, crawled into my day clothes, grabbed my fishing gear, and left the house to walk alone in the cold darkness toward the railway station. I traveled twenty minutes down the line to Como Pier on Sydney's south side. I cast my line and waited.

I had caught a lot of fish in my time, although they were all pretty small. Some men once told me that my tackle was too small, and that is why I never caught anything really big. Believing them, for a time I went fishing with a hook that would make even Moby Dick break into a sweat. And I caught no fish at all.

Sometime after five in the morning, just as the sun was about to rise over the hills, the line in my hand went taut and hard as fencing wire. The pull of the line toward the water was so strong that the nylon started to slip between my fingers. I could hardly believe it. As I followed the line into the water, I could see its entry point darting and circling across the surface as if I had hooked a crazed shark. My heart pounded and leapt into my throat. All I could think was, My God, it must be a bloody whale. What if I lose it? What if I lose it? Please, don't let me lose it!

Gradually and slowly I wound my line around its plastic reel. Bit by bit, I could feel the fish come slowly closer to the surface. Soon I would see it—as long as its frenzy did not wrap the line around the bollards of the pier. *Please not the bollards! At least let me get a glimpse of the monster for my birthday*, I thought to myself. And then, at last, I could see it. A silver bream, maybe two pounds in weight.

It swam this way and that. I could see its beautiful silver scales and its full size in the infant morning light. Then in an instant it was flapping about in the air with my heart flapping alongside it. And then *bang*! There it lay on the deck of the pier with me!

Patterns of Custom and Solicitation

Two pounds at least, I swear, not an ounce less. It might have even been more. I quickly disgorged the hook and put the fish in a small flour bag I had brought with me for more modest game. I sat back euphoric. What a fish! What a catch! What incredible luck!

That day, I first understood what joy was. I sat on the pier, alone, for a few minutes more. I looked around at the quiet river and the brightening sky. Then I packed up all my gear and left immediately. Any more fishing that morning would have felt greedy, ungrateful. A man even asked to buy my fish from me on the return train journey home. Imagine that—an offer to buy my happiness. How often in life do you get an offer like that?

Catching the fish flooded my emotions for days afterward. Even a half century later, I can write about it like it happened only yesterday. Was it because it was the first time I caught a big fish? Was it because it was my birthday? Was it because I felt really, really lucky that day?

Not exactly. What made that concordance of events—big fish, birthday, sense of luck—work together to produce their effects on me was their collective signal. What they *meant* to me. This fishing trip changed the way I saw my life at that time, and it has stayed with me ever since.

Up to that point in my life, my mother and I had struggled as a single-parent family with little support. We always had a sense that opportunities for our happiness and betterment would come from the whims and castoffs of the social world outside us. Mom might get a better job. A relative might feel unexpectedly kindly toward us and invite us to dinner or a party. Friends might invite us to join them on a vacation. Mom might get a pay rise. We might win the lottery. Some great news might come in the post.

The fish that came into my life on my birthday gave me three precious gifts. First, it taught me that unexpected things happen, and some of these can be fantastic. Second, not everything wonderful comes from the world of people. The rest of the material universe may offer you things you need too. And third, though you may *expect* little in this life, *your own actions* can put you in front of possibility and surprise. From there, abundance may be just a short distance away.

These three ideas changed me. Not the fish. Not the birthday. But my-effort-to-catch-the-great-fish-on-my-birthday-alone-on-a-beautiful-morning-with-a-man-trying-to-buy-my-prize-afterward. It was the occurrence of these events together with my thoughts about my life at the time that brought a critical step change to my thinking. This experience is not well served by characterizing it as an incident but rather a convergence of experience. In this way, small incidents that are life changing are nearly always hiding a larger convergence, a larger, deeper, wider story. In this precise way, small incidents can change a life. The world looked different to me after that day. Perhaps I was not transformed, but I was definitely reoriented.

And this appears to be what happens to most people who receive a visit from their dead or their being-of-light friends. It is not the material arrival of the fish alone that necessarily brings the change, but what people make of the appearance of the fish in their lives, often at important times for their inner life.

Though we have just begun to build some very basic data sets about deathbed visions (DBVs)—first through convenience sampling[2] and later somewhat more systematically—we have known for millennia that many dying people see their dead, are often quite happy about it, and die not merely "well" but sometimes quite happily. The psychiatrist Peter Fenwick and colleagues describe a DBV told to them by an interviewee about her mother's last couple of days:

> Suddenly she looked up at the window and seemed to stare intently up at it. . . . She suddenly turned to me and said, "Please, Pauline, don't ever be afraid of dying. I have seen a beautiful light and I was going towards it. . . . It was so peaceful I really had to fight to come back." The next day when it was time for me to go

home I said, "Bye, mum, see you tomorrow." She looked straight at me and said, "I'm not worried about tomorrow, and you mustn't be, promise me." Sadly, she died the next morning ... but I knew she had seen something that day which gave her comfort and peace when she knew she had only hours to live.[3]

Facing one's death is complex emotional, social, and spiritual business. Many people become unconscious hours or days before they actually die. Many others struggle with fear or pain depending on their medical circumstances. To die "in comfort and peace" is no easy task, and this raises the question about what special personal resource a dying person must draw on to achieve such a thing.

What we see in the above case is the encounter with a light again—a simple encounter that seemed wordless. Yet, this experience of light meant far more than its simple description, infusing the percipient with a strength, an insight, or an equanimity that belies that simple description. The encounter with this light not only helped transform her; it reoriented her expectations for tomorrow in a way the narrator could merely guess at.

The encounter occurred inside a larger context of the dying experience itself. It occurred, most likely, inside a soliloquy—an ongoing internal dialogue with her self about what these last days and hours might mean. Her encounter with the light was either the outcome or the additional input that permitted a reformulation of her situation. When the dying behave this way and then die hours later, it is difficult to gather more details of the effect on the percipient. We know a little more from those who have had near-death experiences (NDEs).

The NDE literature is replete with discussions about the transformative effects of the experience[4]—specifically about the aftereffects of meeting beings of light or one's recent or long-dead familiars. The British psychologist Margot Grey cites the following example: "I think I'm still working on what happened, but I just know I have to be a different kind of person; my view of other people has changed. I have always been a very closed and private person, but this experience has made me open up quite a bit. I feel more loving and more involved with people."[5] The pioneer researcher of NDEs Ken Ring cites the story of a survivor of a serious car accident, a young man who describes a new awareness about life:

> There is more going on in life than just the physical part of it.... It was just a total awareness of not just the material and how much we can buy—in the way of cars and stuff, or food or anything. There's more than just consuming life. There's a point where you have to give to it, and that's real important. And there was an awareness at that point that I had to give more of myself out of life. That awareness has come to me.[6]

In her book *Otherworld Journeys*, the religious studies scholar Carol Zaleski provides a more dramatic and reflective account of the changes in those who brush with death, and their own great fish:

> The part of my story that's important is not so much the experience.... What matters most is how my life has changed as a result.... Prior to the experience I didn't feel like I should be alive. After the experience I knew I was *supposed* to be alive. It was a vague feeling, but I knew. I believe the experience was given to me to help me get on the right road, to help me see I am valuable and I should be helping people. And that's what I'm doing through my AA involvement and through my job.[7]

There is little doubt that much of this reorienting and transforming effect has to do with simply being near death itself. However, in studies that have compared those who have had close encounters with death through accidents, falls, or serious illness with and without NDEs, those with them have stronger and longer positive aftereffects. This suggests that the "mystical" dimension of the experience in general, and the deeper and detailed experiences specifically (encounters with dead beings and their familiars), may be crucial to the depth and longevity of those changes.[8]

The bereaved who experience visits from their dead also experience serious changes to their values, beliefs, or outlooks after a postmortem visit. Many of the Guggenheims' respondents claim, for example, that they felt different, better, more positive, and more confident in their subsequent approach to life.[9] Consider these three interview snippets:

> That kind of eased me up a little bit, and I've gained a little more will to live. Now I feel things will get better and I can go along. There must be life after death, since that happened so plain to me.[10]

> When I woke up, I knew in the core of my being that I had just had a reunion with my grandmother! Baba came across time, space, and the universe to tell me she was so happy for me. I felt at peace and had no worries or fears or doubts about going back to the seminary [something he had postponed before this experience].[11]

> It was not as if Kathy was leaving me—it was as though she was in the light, she was the light, and there were no bounds to that light. The light radiated from her to me, and the experience of that light would never leave because now it is a part of me—there was no sense of loss.[12]

All three sources dramatically underline insights about the potential power of a brief incident in life. A small encounter can indeed transform or reorient the person at the center of it. In the specific context of visits from our dead, these are invariably positive (if not immediately, then slowly afterward), and these changes are commonly alterations to one's sense of personal hope and optimism, and openness toward others and the future, even if, counterintuitively, that future seems inevitably bleak—as when facing death. What social or personal processes could possibly account for such major changes, wrought by such small events, inside such difficult mortal circumstances?

Rites of Passage

The Dutch anthropologist Arnold van Gennep wrote the foundational work on the power of ritual on social and personal transformation, entitled *The Rites of Passage*.[13] Van Gennep was among the first to distill a taxonomy from the diversity of human ceremony across cultures.

He observed a pattern of functions across three major phases: an initial period where the novitiate separates from his or her usual identity; a follow-on period where the novitiate is in an in-between space (a period van Gennep called liminality); and the final stage, where the novitiate arrives at a new status and identity through incorporation. These periods literally translate from the French as "transition"—as in "rites of transition"—but in conventional anthropological circles most people retain van Gennep's preference for the term *passage*.[14]

In simple terms, van Gennep was interested in mapping how societies offered a set of controls for crisis and change among themselves. When a baby is born, a wife becomes a mother and a husband becomes a father. At puberty a boy becomes a man, becomes sexually active, and becomes available for marriage. And later a man becomes a husband and a woman a wife. Warriors become elders, and workers become retired. The old and their supporters prepare them and themselves for a coming death. And at death an old man, my father, my son's grandfather, becomes a spirit, an ancestor, a totem. Ceremonies with their supporting myths—or cultural storylines—are the mechanics of how each of us be/come, literally come into being.

In traditional societies, it is easy to understand how one transitions from man to husband or woman to wife. You simply get married. The marriage ceremony has a whole set of storylines both religious and folkloric, and the rites support and are supported by those storylines. But what happens to a society when such rites and stories no longer have this transformative power? What happens when that power, if it remains in place, is weakened? What happens if the rites and storylines do not closely match the personal experience of the initiate? Even in 1960, when Solon Kimball wrote the introduction to *The Rites of Passage* for a new American audience, this was already under way.

> The critical problems of becoming male or female, of relations within the family, and of passing into old age are directly related to the devices which the society offers to the individual to help him achieve the new adjustment. Somehow we seem to have forgotten this—or perhaps the ritual has become so completely individualistic that it is now found for many only in the privacy of the psychoanalyst's couch.[15]

Hunter-gatherer worlds that are populated by spirits, including the spirits of the dead, are the same worlds that offer an arsenal of ritual devices to deal with the restless, vengeful, or ardent dead. Agrarian worlds populated by visiting devils, angels, eccentric saints, or holy visions often come with an equally strong professional services sector to deal with them. It was, and in some places continues to be, the case that clerics offered a full pest control service for beleaguered parishioners. For many of us in the industrial West, it has not been this way for a long time. The world of postmodernity is far less certain, and there are few road maps to guide us through this uncertainty.

Transformation

People marry not once but many times. Or they do not marry at all and have a succession of "partners" throughout life. More and more, many people live alone. Sexual identity is fluid; the strong personal and cultural identity and divisions now seriously blur. Not entirely heterosexual, not always bisexual, not always male or female, not every day anyway. Gender and sexuality are contingent, ambiguous, contested, and changeable. People give birth when they are young, or old, or not even female, or not fertile. People have not one but many careers—or none. Alternative lifestyles are not confined to self-sufficiency in food and energy consumption but now include choices about work and partnering lifestyles, or religious and political choices. And entering into these current and evolving complexities is an old, long-standing, and cross-cultural visitor—the merry dead.

It seems, at least on the face of it, that there are no strong rites of passage that permit us to process these visits. In the West we have a set of gradual social rites of separation for our dying: retirement, ocean cruising, and endless golf. But this does not apply to all the elderly, and certainly does not apply to those who die in accidents or from serious illness early in life. In intensive care contexts, there are instances of vigils by families that morph into wakes of a brief sort before becoming funerals. Some of these funerals may be traditional while others are not. There are no bereavement rites that translate this motley and diverse set of separation and liminal experiences felt by survivors into final experiences of psychological resolution and group incorporation.

This lack of rites has been a long-standing social criticism as well as an anthropological and psychiatric observation. And to be fair to the theory of rites of passage, not all rites exercise their functions equally anyway. In funeral rites, for example, the rites of separation tend to be more prominent than the other functions, such as liminality or incorporation. In betrothal or pregnancy, the rites of liminality are more prominent than functions like separation or incorporation.

Whether or not we have adequate modern rites and functions to reincorporate the bereaved, the dead should have a parallel set of rites. The bereaved must be encouraged back to the living, and the dead must be encouraged not to hang around. The rites of passage in human societies are traditionally designed to cater to both audiences—the bereaved and the dead. Currently we have little provision for either of these groups.

We have, for the most part, supplanted historical traditions with personal biography. Our society does not prescribe our life course anymore; it only circumscribes it, through law, work cultures, and state regulation. The rest of our lives—our choice of mate, elective reproduction, career, religious or recreational activities, and so on—is now simply subject to personal aspiration, felt need, or ambition, all constrained by the usual suspects of social determination: wealth, age, gender, or education. Unlike traditional Melanesian or Polynesian society, our society has no laws covering who to marry, the order of ceremonies at an initiation into manhood, or what to do during unexpected appearances of your dead. We are on our own. Biography is our only guide.

As I observed earlier in this book, most people who have not encountered their dead reach for the two popular scripts. The first is New Age philosophies that encompass bits of Eastern religion and Western Spiritualism and paganism. The second is rational humanism or its subgenre of pop psychology or an overweaned attachment to Western empirical science. However, for people visited by the dead or beings of light, this does not help them explain their experience. It creates an environment of reticence to share their experience for fear of stigma or character assassination or distortion. And it imposes an impersonal framework on a very personal event.

Current cultural scripts position the experiencer-percipient as deluded or as someone at the mercy of their own biology. Visits from the dead are like being prone to epileptic seizures. You cannot help it. If it keeps happening, you might need to see someone in the therapeutic professions, maybe get some medication. The alternative is to go have your aura read or read one of the countless books that argue that there is no death. (It is interesting to note that none of these books are written by funeral directors or homicide detectives.) For countless numbers of people today, these are fairly impoverished choices, uncomfortable choices, underwhelming and unhelpful choices, none of which speak to what happened. Frankly, they are no choices at all.

Instead, most people tend to look to their biographies. Maybe their unexpected and surprising visits speak to their experience as a whole. In other words, does the encounter make overall sense to their journey so far, and this particular part of their life specifically? It is these questions, then, that go to the very heart of, if not a rite of passage, the maturity of experience that ripens a person for passage. Or to put it another way, readying them for change at that precise time. Keeping this in mind, let us look again at accounts of visitations that do not describe the actual visit at all.

From Sally's story from chapter 4:

At the time of her death I had a lot going on, including considerable family fall out and trying to raise a five-year-old daughter as a single mum. Then a funny thing happened, and as I mentioned, a lot was going on in my life then. One night, a month or two after Nan died, not long after I had gone to bed . . .

From Katherine Russell Rich not long after she was diagnosed with breast cancer:

In November, a curious thing happened. On the night before my thirty-third birthday, I was lying in bed, face to the wall, crying. Despondence had burned off the Scotch I'd drunk, and was now propelling me into hysteria. Between sobs, I'd go rigid, and it was in one of those moments of silence that I sensed a presence in the room behind me. Startled, I turned my head and saw . . . [16]

Or consider this complete case from Barry, a bereaved man recalling a powerful dream where he meets his dead grandfather:

> My grandpa died like ten years ago in an accident, and a few years ago I was going through a really rough patch in my life. One night I went to sleep feeling distressed like my life was falling apart and in my dream I was in this really clean empty town where all the buildings look the same and led myself to a building with bright white halls and into a bright white room (I thought it was like a giant lab but giant library is fitting too) with twin sized beds next to each other.[17]

Next he describes the incident:

> My grandpa was laying on one and told me to lay down in the other one. When my grandpa was alive, we didn't really communicate verbally very well because we spoke different languages but we loved each other. In this dream, he spoke to me, not verbally or in a language but like in a mental conversation and it was very fluid (it's hard to explain). We were lying next to each other and I'm pouring out to him how scared and lonely I am. He looks over to me and told me I don't need to fear anything because I am always being guided and cared for by him and "others" no matter what I choose in my life. I can't see it but if I try, I can always feel that I'm loved.

Then his incident ends, and his story rejoins the context of the opening: "When I woke up I felt so warm and peaceful."[18]

What is immediately striking about these three cases is the comments about biographical context. You cannot help but see how each of these percipients draws on his or her strange encounter to reanalyze and reformulate immediate past problems and challenges. Their visitors are there to address an issue within the life of the percipient. This is neither a ghost story nor a boogeyman story. Instead, the percipients see the visitors as players with a quite specific role. And while this is largely self-evident in these three accounts, it often is not in many others, especially in accounts of visions told by the bereaved.

Why is this context so commonly ignored? It appears to be the popular obsession with the details of the actual visit. Many published presentations of an encounter with dead familiars are offered to readers without their context—an omission is as simple as it is regrettable.

A narrow focus on the content of the vision from a psychology, parapsychology, or medical gaze tends to filter out the context, often selling short the context in the manufacture of meaning. Sometimes, overly influenced by the dominant cultural context, experiencers will do this to themselves. They will inadvertently self-censor. Because the emphasis of these genres of commentary has been less interested in meaning-making and more interested in what caused the encounter, many examples of visions of the bereaved (VBs) are quoted without biographical context. At other times, the storyteller will omit these details of personal context *because* they are so personal.

And yet it is this very context that the bereaved employ to make sense of the encounter and to fuel their personal transformation. This is less an omission in DBVs or NDEs. For some reasons, VBs are commonly presented as literature closely allied to ghost stories. The emphasis is on the incident and not the biography, yet it is biography that matters most in understanding how these encounters change us.

In DBVs, the story is always told in the context of someone who is self-evidently dying. Nevertheless, this context is used partly to explain how the physical dying process may be responsible for the "unusual" encounters and rarely, if ever, used to link biographical rupture and crisis to the perception of new experiences. In NDEs, a similar process occurs, and once again, dying is often used to "explain" why these encounters with the dead or beings of light occur. Because most narratives about NDEs often posit being near death as a prerequisite (it is not, as VBs will attest), biographical context is a specific battleground for epistemological wars about the nature of reality, consciousness, and psychopharmacy.

The events leading up to the medical crisis, or the effects of the medical crisis or accident on a person who remains aware during the ordeal, are rarely, if ever, employed as a possible causal factor. And while many NDE books showcase how the experience transformed their recipients' lives, the emphasis is firmly on the actual mystical content and not the interplay between that content and their lives up to that point. The long-term academic and clinical analysis has been psychological and not sociological.

If one views the powerful reorientation effect of encounters with the dead out of context, we see major transformations arising from events lasting some seconds or minutes. But in fact, and in context, these personal changes derive from both negative and positive forces in a person's life that have occurred over many months, sometimes even years. The context may be the cause of the encounter or the crucial prompt to its reevaluation, but overall the incident qua incident has little lasting meaning as a personal compass. Any incident understood outside its specific context is merely a narrative shell, serviceable only to paranormal advocates and skeptics alike as they beat their political drums.

I HAVE ALREADY DESCRIBED how the modern cultural context has moved us away from a tribal society where our life course is determined by fixed and unchanging social positions of gender, social class, caste, age, and family. In a traditional society, one's life chances were heavily constrained by folk traditions, religions, and laws that governed every aspect of personal lifestyle and choice.

In the contemporary West, people are largely free to make their own way in life, and this usually means that the construction of their self is a personal project—something to mold and change with different values and experiences influenced by educational opportunities, travel, social networks, and experiences. In the postmodern world, "me" is a project to be crafted and developed throughout the life course. It is not, as it had been for most of human history, inherited and unchangeable, something that takes its place in a fixed and predetermined social order.

This means that most people are now open to influence, to a new argument, to a new book, to a new friendship or club or career change. But it also means more uncertainty, instability, and an equal chance of events going wrong. Though life expectancy has never been higher on earth for most humans, still children die, adolescents commit suicide, parents are killed in work accidents, and people get cancer or have heart attacks. Marriages fail, and fail repeatedly. People are fired or go bankrupt. Life has never been freer, but with this freedom comes great uncertainty and vulnerability. Boredom is now less a problem than personal crisis and unhappiness. As Henry David Thoreau once observed, the mass of people "lead lives of quiet desperation."[19]

In this unsettling sociological context, most people are also quietly looking for any guidance they can get. Look again at my own reflections about my great fish moment:

> Up to that point in my life, my mother and I had struggled as a single-parent family with little support and opportunity. We always had a sense that opportunities for our happiness and betterment would come from the whims and castoffs of the social world outside us. Mom might get a better job. A relative might feel unexpectedly kindly toward us and invite us to dinner or a party. Friends might invite us to join them on a vacation. Mom might get a pay rise. We might win the lottery. There might be some great news coming in the post.
>
> The fish that came into my life on my birthday gave me three precious gifts. First, it taught me that unexpected things happen, and some of these can be fantastic. Second, not everything wonderful comes from the world of people. The rest of the material

universe may offer you things you need too. And third, though you may *expect* little in this life, *your own actions* can put you in front of possibility and surprise. From there, abundance may be just a short distance away.

What do you see here? You see someone—a twelve-year-old—formulating and manufacturing values about how to act in the future because of a fishing trip. Perhaps this was necessary because I had no father to bounce these ideas off, and at that stage of my life that left a real hole. I had no paternal figure to socialize me with a useful attitude or values that would help me with my childish experiences of despair or vulnerability.

If I had had a father at that time, maybe I would have a life-changing story about an exchange I had with him during a fishing trip and not simply an account of my own soliloquy as influenced by catching a surprisingly big fish on my birthday. And to extend this speculation one step further, this account might then have sounded a bit like Barry's: "We were lying next to each other and I'm pouring out to him how scared and lonely I am. He looks over to me and told me I don't need to fear anything because I am always being guided and cared for by him and 'others' no matter what I choose in my life. I can't see it but if I try, I can always feel that I'm loved."[20]

Perhaps our visitors transform and reorient us because as a modern people we are open to change. No longer guided or directed by tradition, we are currently built for that very purpose of openness. And the support we need for reorientation, especially in times of trouble or sadness—whether this is while dying or while grieving—comes optimally from people we trust, living or dead. It is difficult, and often very difficult, to find that kind of guidance when we need it. Everyone knows that. So when it comes, it feels much like a kind of *gift*. But what do we mean by gift?

7

Gifts

LIKE MOST BABY BOOMERS, I have had my share of close friends and family die. In 2016, one of my closest friends died of lung cancer.

Roy and I met when we were sixteen years old. We went to different schools but I was dating his cousin at the time. From then on we were the closest of buddies. Even though after high school Roy went to work in a factory and I went to college, our friendship never faltered. I made friends with his friends from his work, and he made friends with my university pals. No one ever thought that much about our different occupational backgrounds. We were just "Al and Roy" to my friends and "Roy and Al" to his.

Eventually I became a professor, and Roy simply acknowledged that it must be a good thing to be one of those and left it at that. We never much talked about our different occupations, except to occasionally grumble about them. We had a kind of mutual understanding. We came from the same place, both teenagers from the working class, from a similar migrant background, who grew up together in the same neighborhood. We had the same view of politics, football, and girls. But most of all, Roy was just the kindest and most patient person alive. When I got married, Roy was like a brother, not just to me but to my wife too. Both of quiet and reserved disposition in public, they also instinctively understood each other.

I always thought that if anyone died and came back to see me, it would be Roy. But so far he has not.

The Swiss American psychiatrist Elisabeth Kübler-Ross, whose book *On Death and Dying*[1] rocketed her to fame in the 1970s, spent her career as I have spent mine, talking and writing about dying. Toward the end of her career, she boasted about being contacted by her dead former patients, and quite often too. Much of her writing about those experiences brought her public scorn and discredit. For the medical community in particular, she became an embarrassment.

I remember that time and those writings well. I felt sorry for Elizabeth then, as I do now. Not because I thought she had slipped a cognitive disc, but because the ridicule and rejection were largely a response from a rather conservative time when topics like death and dying were only just emerging as things we could talk about. Near-death experiences (NDEs) and visions of the bereaved (VBs) were widely viewed as freak phenomena, almost certainly psychiatric in nature. Her comfort with these topics appeared to many to be, as they say, really *out there*. But now, looking back on my thirty years of working among the dying, I often find myself wondering why Elizabeth saw so many of her dead former patients and I have never seen even one. Lately I have wondered why I have not seen Roy again.

Now, let me say at this point that I have no beliefs about the afterlife. But neither do I dismiss the possibility. I have heard a lot of provocative and evocative stories from patients, families, clinical colleagues, and academic colleagues. I know the literature of mystical and altered states of consciousness—more than well enough to knock the arrogance out of most people. But let me pause here to say, in a rather prosaic way, that if you were to choose the person most likely to give a fair reception to such an experience, wouldn't you think of me? So where the hell are you, Roy?

But in 2018, something happened that changed all that. And it came from an unexpected place. In Australia, the wife of another close childhood friend of mine died. Heather had a late diagnosed, advanced metastatic cancer. She died within a year of finding out. I had known Heather since she was eighteen, when she first met my friend Jake. From that time on, I was friends with both of them, although I tended to see more of Jake. But they were both very old friends who had visited my wife and me over the years, and we them, even though we were overseas for the past fourteen years. When Heather died, I was already en route to Australia.

Jake picked me up at the airport. He had booked a motel room for me along with rooms for his adult daughter and son. His house was already filled with other relatives and friends who had arrived earlier. Jake was in pretty sad shape, although he was holding up well and had made all the relevant funeral arrangements, in addition to accommodating and entertaining the large incoming group of mourners.

It was about nine at night when we finally arrived at the motel. Jake and I went to the reception desk and spoke with the attendant. She gave us the key, and Jake suggested I check out my room to make sure I was happy with everything. He would wait at the reception desk in case there was any problem. If everything was OK, he would pick me up in front of my room and we would drive back to his house.

I walked to my room and dropped off my stuff, then walked back out to the porch, closing the door behind me. I waited for Jake in the dark. I could see his car parked in front of the reception office, a stone's throw from where I stood.

I was tired and a bit jet-lagged from my long trip from England. I looked up at the sky and some of the trees around me in a sort of distracted reverie. Australia always feels so warm and humid to me compared with England, no matter the season. And the trees and flowers were so lush and fragrant in this northern part of New South Wales that evening.

I meditated on being home again. I saw Jake's headlights come on, and I heard the wheels quietly crunching over the gravel. And then it happened.

A spreading excitement moved over my chest and quickly spread to my shoulders. It continued upward into my neck, then into my head. It took only a couple of seconds for this wave to flood my senses. I felt bolted to the ground, immobilized, but also weirdly thrilled, swooning momentarily in a kind of drunken joy, even, dare I say, an ecstasy of sorts.[2]

Jake was driving slowly toward me. Suddenly, in this tingling, flooding sensation of happiness came a message inside my head. Not words, not even a voice. Just an explicably clear message, which I immediately understood.[3] It did not even come to me in sequence but rather all at once. And I knew it was from Heather.

I realize that reads a bit wacky, for which I apologize. But that is how it was. The message was this: "I'm happy. I'm glad you two are together again. Tell him."

I knew the happiness that I had felt was actually hers. Jake stopped the car in front of me and waited. The feelings of joy receded, and the stiffness began to melt away. When I got into the car, Jake asked me if the room was OK. I said it was, and I said no more as we drove away in silence.

I was so shaken by the experience that I could not share it right away. To say I was unsettled does not do the experience justice. I was amazed. I just could not make heads or tails of what had just happened, even though, at the same time, my academic work has prepared me for the obvious explanation. My experience had the hallmark features of a vision of bereavement except for visual apparition—the emotional sensation, the wordless greeting, the directive, the ineffable mode of communication but with clarity of message and purpose notwithstanding. It was obvious that I had received a message from Heather. How the hell is this going to go down with Jake? I decided I needed time to process this and probably brace myself for a critical reaction. I said nothing about this to Jake during my whole time in Australia.

After I returned to England, I reviewed my own biopsychological options, as one does. Like Scrooge encountering Marley in Charles Dickens's *A Christmas Carol*, I wondered whether I had eaten something that did not agree with me.[4] Or had I drunk any alcohol beforehand? Or had I been under any extraordinary stress other than what is typical for international flights? But I could not honestly say yes to any of these.

A month later I told Jake about the experience. He had mixed feelings about the story. He trusted me. He knows I am not a liar or a drunk or a junkie. He knows very well what I do for a living and my specialty within hospice care. But in the end, the best response he could come up with was that he thought I might have imagined it and that he wished it could have been him.

This chapter does not theorize why I received the communication and Jake did not. Instead, it is about the gifts given by the dead.

I felt I had been given a gift from Heather. I do not know why she communicated with me but Roy did not. I do not know why I have not had dozens of communications from dead people like lucky Elizabeth, but I was pleased to have something in my life that I absolutely felt was a genuine communication from someone dead and that felt as real as any other waking experience I have ever had. It gave me firsthand experience of two things I had only ever read about as a mere academic: the stigma and rejection that come when you disclose a personal mystical experience, and wordless communication.

Heather made me realize that personal experience does not provide any significant advantage over academic experience when it comes to telling other people. In fact, it is probably a disadvantage.

Academic knowledge is supposed to be impersonal and thus credible, ergo personal experience is *in*credible. Telling my friend about an incident that he identified with a preposterous realm gave me firsthand experience of what the psychologist Judith Posner calls "a courtesy stigma"—those who associate with a stigmatized idea attract the same stigma.[5]

I at last felt linked with my childhood piano teacher who saw her dead mother in her lounge some fifty years earlier. Our mutual lesson in humility was to realize that experience—no matter how amazing—may not always beget belief. Like my piano teacher, I have not become a believer in the afterlife, but the experience has strengthened my determination to reinforce the social science door against those who would close it on an important and widespread human experience.

Transactions

When I examine the idea that the dead bring gifts, I come up with three possibilities. First, the gift I received from Heather may have been Heather's real intention—she was offering me something I could use. Or, second, it may not have been her direct intention but it was definitely one of the effects. Or, and linked to this second observation, the gift may simply be my interpretation. In all these possibilities, the result is the same. Heather gave me a personal experience that will be an ongoing source of inspiration. The dead bring gifts. But how common is this type of social transaction between the dead and the living?

The idea that the dead bring gifts is partly an extension of the earlier observation that the dead and their being-of-light friends come with advice and direction. Sometimes, though, the offerings they bring are more unobtrusive, as they were in my case. Heather brought me the gift of something quite personal to underscore that my academic work had something to check against in a living sense. These kinds of gifts are offered up in the currencies of reassurance, creative stimulus, support, comfort, or even simple companionship.

Heather's communication with me, in the context of bereavement, is pretty typical of a lot of bereavement communication and subsequent interpretation. I am not the only one to characterize this abrupt and unusual experience as "inspirational." A more famous example comes from Paul McCartney, and how he "had a dream in the '60s where my mum, who died, came to me in the dream and was reassuring me, saying, 'It's going to be OK, just let it be.' She gave me the positive word. So I woke and went: 'What was that? What'd she say? Let it be? I've never heard that. That's kind of good.'"[6] In a similar story of inspiration gifted by a dead friend, in 1982 a young woman named Sheila Gibbons entered college and met her new best friend, Angela. Two years later, Angela was murdered. Since Sheila knew most of the people that Angela knew, she helped police investigate. It was, according to Sheila, the most traumatic time in her life, and she left college soon after.

Sheila continued to help the police with their inquiries, but they were not able to solve Angela's murder. Eventually Sheila got married, changed her name to Sheila Wysocki, had children, and moved away. Then one evening in 2004, Sheila recalls:

> I was doing Bible study homework. I dreaded doing it. Whoever designed it did not design it for someone who's dyslexic—small print, close together, very tight—it's torture for me to read.
>
> So I was reading and then I remember looking to the right and there was Angie. I thought, "Am I dreaming? Am I asleep? What is it?"
>
> There was no talking, it was just her and her great smile.
>
> I don't know if I believe in ghosts, but I have a lot of faith and I believe that there are messages, and at that moment I thought,

"It's time." I leaned over to my nightstand and picked up the phone and called the Dallas Police Department, just like that.[7]

This critical incident led Sheila to train as a private detective, badger the police department in Dallas, form a partnership with a homicide officer there, and solve her friend's murder. It turns out that the man who murdered her friend was a serial rapist and killer, and today he sits on death row.

These are strange incidents to be sure. But whatever their source, the social transaction that they engender fits into a broader cross-cultural pattern—the exchange of gifts. It is for *that* reason that the interactions occur in the very way that they do. We are given something to take with us. It is the same kind of offering made to those who are near death. In deathbed studies I conducted with medical colleagues in India[8] and in the Republic of Moldova in Eastern Europe,[9] these are the gifts described by family and by the dying people in their care.

As noted earlier, in both of these studies the general prevalence of deathbed visions (DBVs) is about 30 percent. In the Moldovan study, family commonly reported that the dying person felt supported or "assisted" in some way by the visions: "He dreamed that his dead mother had come through the door. It happened in the last few days, he spoke often about this and would say that his mother was coming to get him. He would ask if I could see her too, he was saying this with his eyes open, he would say a few times a day that his mother had come."[10] Other dying people spoke about the comfort that they had received in communications with their dead:

> Before he died, we were all in the house together. I was at his feet. At this time he turned his head toward the wall and it was though he was talking to someone and he said, "No worries, everything will be all right. Everything will be enough, it will be good and beautiful. . . ." We didn't know who he spoke to and we don't know what he meant either. But he told our daughter Svetlana—

she is our second daughter—"Be aware that everything will be on your shoulders."[11]

For other dying people, visits from the dead provided them with companionship. Sometimes the visitors were intimates such as parents, and other times they were former friends and villagers. "I don't know if she had 'visions' but she would often be in a trance when she spoke to my father, who was dead, or with my mother (likewise, she had been dead many years), and she would also speak to a child." And again: "Yes, he had visions. He would look out of the window and call people who were already dead to come to him inside the house. He would tell me he could see them looking at him. He saw several dead people. He practically listed all our neighbors and relatives who had long died."[12] Many dying people within these studies claimed to see and talk with their dead and to receive important gifts from them: comfort, support, companionship. Others spoke about these visits more tangibly as gifts of reunion—of seeing long-dead loved ones once more before they die. They enjoyed their reunion and often spoke of it as a gift in itself. Sometimes, the dead bring specific insights, such as a prognosis, especially if the dying person has not been told of their mortal prospects. The following case is a good example of the type of informational gift received from one's dead companions:

> He dreamed about my mother, who had already died and whom he missed. He had been extraordinarily fond of her. He also dreamed about my brother, who died suddenly at the age of thirty-two; he had a heart attack and died within half an hour. Father dreamed about both of them, they seemed to be dancing happily at a wedding and they called him. He then told me, "They will take me away with them." I tried to console him, told him it would not happen, that he would get well . . . but he said he would die, that I had done everything for him. . . . He had that dream about one month before he died.[13]

Sometimes, talking with your dead can give you a sense of control or choice. One family member describes an account of a DBV where choice was exercised rather vigorously:

> And I noticed during the day that he was talking to dead people, he had visions. When he recovered from those states, he would tell me his relatives who had already died had come to see him, they would grab him and take him somewhere but he would resist. He told me he held on to the pole outside the house, with difficulty, but he did not leave with them.[14]

The word *gift* is used over and over by people all over the world who have been through all sorts of NDEs. Some report that returning to life itself was a gift. Others report their reorientation toward life—a greater interest in learning, of human service, or of spiritual matters. And others report that they are now "different" as human beings—they have greater human sensitivities, such as a bit of clairvoyance or telepathy or a sense of great connection with the natural and social worlds. Some speak about losing their fear of death as a gift. In fact, the idea is so common in the literature that we see it often in articles and books in the genre: "Amazing Grace: The Near-Death Experience as Compensatory Gift,"[15] *Final Gifts: Understanding the Special Awareness, Needs, and Communications of the Dying,*[16] or *The Gifts of the Near-Death Experience.*[17]

A nineteen-year-old describes the gift he feels he has received from nearly drowning and encountering a being of light:

> Almost ten years later, while under the influence of psychedelic mushrooms, I recalled my near-death experience (for which I had only recently discovered the name and that there were others who had had similar experiences) and realized the tremendous impact it had on my life ... my sense of spirituality, my interest in exploring different states of consciousness, my reverence for nature, my passion for environmental and social justice, just about every-

thing! It felt as though it completely marked the trajectory of my life.[18]

Another teenager describes how the social counters experienced in NDEs became the main guiding influence in her life:

> My very personal experience of and relationship with this light brings me untold comfort, and motivates me to do good in this world. I feel more empathetic with others than before, and less judgmental. I realize, now more than ever, that kindness and helping others is a direct manifestation of the Light, and the best we can do in this world is to multiply the incandescence of God here on Earth. It feeds our soul, and the souls of others. Why else would we be here, in this flimsy and imperfect place? Suffering exists to give us a chance to overcome and to grow. To create something beautiful out of something ugly is the ultimate gratification.[19]

In all the above cases—from NDEs to DBVs to VBs—the dead or their being-of-light friends come to offer gifts of support, comfort, reunion, companionship, choice and control, inspiration, or desire for action, whether that is exemplified in a subsequent career change, new learning, spirituality, biographical insight, or simply a quality of peace at the end of life itself. However, it is important to add that, just as Saul discovered on the road to Damascus, not all encounters—and therefore not all gifts—are nice.

The palliative researcher Robert W. Putsch describes a number of cases from First Nations and Hmong (an ethnic group of East and Southeast Asia) of less desirable visits.[20] A deceased Salish father visited his daughter's bedside to sing a song he thought ought to have been sung for him at his funeral. It was then subsequently sung at his memorial. A dead Hmong father visited his daughter several times with an angry face, especially during her bouts of headache. A family conference concluded that this was because she had not sought his permission to marry. After a series of rites and invocations were made to her deceased parents, the daughter subsequently received another visit—this one from her deceased mother voicing approval; after that, she was never bothered again.

Two observations may be made here. First, although most visits are extremely positive, not all visits by deceased people, especially parents, provide comfort and support. Some visits by the dead reflect old concerns about control and sanction. These are rarely horrible, but neither are they pleasant. Second, and these last cases underline this point better than the more pleasant examples, gifts come with reciprocal obligations.

The gifts that people claim to receive—however subtle or dramatic—are not without strings attached. Reciprocity is in the nature of these gifts. In the world of human history and culture, we "return" or exchange gifts. This is why they appear at all in the social world of human interaction. This anthropological insight is commonly overlooked in the popular, modern impression that gifts are free—with no entailments or obligations. Even the *Oxford English Dictionary* promotes this popular understanding in its assertion that a gift is "a thing given willingly to someone without payment."[21] But that is not the case with most gifts, including the ones we receive from the dead.

Reciprocity

The idea of the gift has a dual meaning. The impression of this double meaning begins almost immediately when we examine its etymology. The word *gift* has long meant "something given," but it also originally meant "poison" ("to give to drink") in early Dutch and German sources, implying that any poison will not only kill its recipient but also beg for an antidote. Even in Old English the cognate word *gift* is related to dowry, a bride price, and other forms of *reciprocal* obligation.[22] Extending and underlining these meanings, the anthropological meaning of gift in its most detailed form comes to us from the work of the French anthropologist Marcel Mauss.[23]

Mauss argued that all gifts are part of a broader obligatory pattern of exchange relations. It is a reciprocal pattern with three key obligations: the obligation to give, the obligation to receive, and the obligation to repay. In its illustration of what it views as an obligation-free gift, the *Oxford English Dictionary* offers the wedding gift as an example. But what kind of wedding guest does not bring a gift? Only a rude or ungrateful one. This is because wedding gifts are always *expected*. You are obliged to gift *in return for the gift of the invitation*. When one receives a gold watch on retirement from work, one might expect that this gift is free from obligation. But even these gifts are offered in repayment for services rendered over many years. Long service is a gift to employers and not an expectation. And even when it is expected, as in Japan, then gifts recognize expectations met. The retirement gift is repayment.

Gifts are never really given away in social relations. Though one might receive a gift from another, which means that the receiver now owns the gift, the spirit of the gift remains with the giver. In this sense, every time one looks at the watch or the wedding gift of champagne flutes, one is reminded of the giver. The spirit of the giver is always present (note the dual meaning here) within the gift. The sociological reason behind this set of object relations is that the memory of the giver in the gift recalls the giver's sacrifice, labor, previous ownership, invention, or design of the gift. Mauss reminds us of the old Chinese custom where a gift giver maintains the right to weep over the object they originally owned as if they owned its essence in perpetuity. Even in the West, we recognize this perpetual essence or spirit of the gift in intellectual property or copyright laws with respect to fair use. Though we may buy and own artwork or a commercial product, the company or the artist retains ownership of the design. You never buy everything about an object in social and economic exchanges.

The custom of gift exchange applies to all major social exchanges across the lifespan in most societies, and this includes the offering of gifts to the dead. Throughout history and most societies, gifts have been offered to our dead to keep them happy, to solicit favors, or to keep them away, and for the purposes of these aims—to oblige them to do so. Human and animal sacrifices, the burnt offerings of furniture or even houses, the performance of extensive ceremonial rites, and the simple offer of prayers are some of the many gifts the living offer up to the dead to either repay debt or solicit their favors. So what was the gift exchange implied by Heather's appearance to me?

Heather offered to me what I interpreted later as a unique and ongoing source of inspiration for my work in this area. She also gave me an exceptional experience in which to ponder not only her own future welfare and whereabouts but possibly my own in the future, in ways more powerful than any book had ever offered me. And in return for this? Whatever her intent (or my subsequent interpretation), my obligation was made absolutely clear—summarized in her explicit final message to me: "Tell him." I am sure Heather knew I would value, perhaps even understand readily, what she was doing. But at the same time, she expected me to get over it and do her bidding. What she asked me to do was simple enough, but it was an *expectation*.

Paul McCartney's mother appeared because she seemed concerned about the worries that were dogging his life. What those were I do not know. Paul, like many people telling a story about bereavement visions, does not reveal the whole of where this encounter fits into his biography at that time. Did he labor under grief for his mother's death for a long time? Did the dream come at a time of particular stress? Clearly she came to reassure him in his dream. The gifts were reassurance and reunion inside this dream. From this encounter, Paul wrote "Let It Be." The gift expectation is implied in this exchange. The directive that came to Paul, less demanding than Heather's command, was to ease up a bit, let things take their course, do not fret, and let it be. That was the expected repayment.

Both Heather and McCartney's mother bore a gift with the expectation of repayment implied in the gift itself. Though both Paul and I received the vision, the vision itself was a gift relation[24] in these examples because the visitors either directed or implied a return offering—in these cases in the form of an expected behavior from myself and Paul. There is an expectation in this transaction: failure to return means wasted energy for the visitor and rudeness or intransigence on behalf of the ones visited. This is the bad wedding guest syndrome. It does not mean we must oblige—and some people would and do ignore the directives or the advice of their dead visitors. But the main task here is to note the ongoing backstory of expectation frequently overlooked in these examples of visionary experience.

The same rules applied to Sheila Wysocki. The message she received was that it was time. But time for what? In the context of the story that Sheila tells us, it was time for her to identify Angela's murderer, as fantastic as that must sound to anyone reading her story. Angela came into her traumatized friend's life just one more time. This was a gift of reassurance, for sure, but, like all gifts, it came with an expectation that Sheila understood immediately. Sheila, Paul McCartney, and I all understood that the gift we received required repayment, that return expectations were attached.

But what about DBVs? Surely there is little or no time for repayment. Before we address this question, let us just step back for a brief moment and remind ourselves what we are doing here. To apply the basic principles of social interaction is to imply that we are not discussing ghost stories or stories about supernatural beings whose motivations are mysterious or secretive. Bereavement or near-death visions are not playful exercises by fickle and capricious Greek gods. Rather, the key to understanding the behavior of dead people is to recognize that they are *people*. They communicate largely within our social rules. Their actions have a rationale, a social reasoning about them—that is, a shared social logic. The dead grew up with and were shaped by our customs and beliefs. If they come back, they do so using those same shared rules. To understand the dead as previously alive friends or relatives, we must consider those rules.

So what do we find in the gift-exchange relationship in DBVs? Comfort, support, companionship, even reunion, and sometimes information about a prognosis. All these are gifts offered up by our dead to our soon-to-be dead. What do they want in return? For many dead companions, they apparently want us to join them, and quickly. A bit scary, sure, but let us look at it another way.

When I was thirteen, I used to visit a beach in eastern Australia. Behind the main beach was a deep tidal lagoon, and behind the lagoon rose a steep cliff about seventy feet high. Kids (and some adults) would jump from the cliff into the lagoon. Now, I do not know if any of you have ever jumped from seventy feet into water, but let me just tell you it is pretty intimidating the first time you try.

Many decide not to do it. Once you are up there, it certainly looks a very long way down. And you are not even sure how deep the water is. It may be shallow enough that you will break your neck, or it may be so deep that the plunge sends you down farther than you can swim. Terrifying. But on a popular weekend, can you guess what happens?

There is a cheer squad down on the beach opposite the other side of the lagoon. Kids—and some adults—look up and egg on the jumpers. They were there when I first tried it. The kids would chant, "Jump, jump, jump!" Some would yell up encouragement, like, "C'mon, it's easy."

When I first heard about the dead visiting the deathbed of the dying, I thought it was ghastly, as though they were ghouls who wanted people to die. But after a few moments of thought, I remembered the cheerleaders on the beach. Just like them, these visitors were cheering on the dying. They knew the dying were going to make the jump eventually, and they were rallying around to aid them.

In the book's opening chapter you can see examples of dying children encouraged by their grandmothers to join them. And you can see examples of people who, despite the encouragement, do not jump, do not oblige. Not everyone who gets a gift returns the favor. Here we recall the Moldovan who complained that his dead friends "would grab him and take him somewhere but he would resist. He told me he held on to the pole outside the house, with difficulty, but he did not leave with them."[25] I have seen exactly this scenario happen at the cliff top at the beach! Here is a man who knows his own mind—he will jump when he is good and ready, thank you very much. Cheering or dragging him to the edge is *not* going to help him!

For those who have had an NDE, the expectations are often as clear and singular as they are for DBVs. When we reconsider the two accounts of the nineteen-year-olds, we are struck by the breadth of the existential lesson. Being "sent back," particularly after interaction with the dead or a being of light who reminds you that you have work to do, implies that you must do that work. It also implies that you must reflect back the messages and experiences gained from that other place, that you better represent that experience in everyday life. For most who brush with NDEs, this has meant a life devoted to more spiritual, learning, and service pursuits, and relationships in the social world and in all of nature itself. The reflections of the two nineteen-year-olds on their NDEs are emblematic of the expectations given to those who have undergone a life-changing event.

When our dead come to see us, they often bring an assortment of services and products—from reassurance and peace to advice and directives. But remember that these are not showered on us like confetti. They come with obligations and expectations, whether we choose to honor them or not. And that is because all gifts have come with these reciprocities since time immemorial. Sometimes the expectations are explicit. Sometimes they are implicit. Sometimes they are veiled backstories that are unknown to a reader or listener. But always, everywhere, and at all times past and present, the dead expect things from us. And so they visit.

PART III

A Pattern Directing the Patterns

8
Vigils

ONCE UPON A TIME, my wife and I were living in a small ten-acre valley surrounded by heavily wooded hills. We lived in a stone house about ninety minutes from Melbourne, Australia. Unusually, our property was surrounded on three sides by national park forests. Opposite us was privately owned pastureland that was part of a grazing property. Our house was so secluded and private—almost a fairy-tale place, really. No neighbors to overlook us, not even close. We lived there quietly, enjoying our seclusion, the peace only occasionally broken by the happy barking of one of our three collies.

One morning I was inside the house, sitting in the dining room reading the paper, when I turned to notice our youngest collie drinking from her water bowl near the kitchen. Just as my gaze settled on her, the window next to her shattered. Our dog hit the floor, legs akimbo. For a second—a terribly long second—I thought she had been shot. She laid on the floor like that for a moment before gathering up her four jellyfish legs and flying up the staircase to lodge a garbled, if somewhat hysterical, complaint to my wife in the bedroom.

A Pattern Directing the Patterns

I walked over to the broken window, and there on the floor among the broken glass was a large, beautiful, but unconscious brown-feathered hawk.

Without a moment to lose, I scooped up the hawk with both hands and ran to the back door. When I got outside, the hawk began to come around. It lifted its head woozily to look at me. I released it into the air with a swift throw forward, and it caught flight—a little zig here and a longer zag there, but off it went more or less in the direction of the nearby woods. When I returned to the house, my shocked collie was standing sheepishly behind my wife. I cleaned up the shattered glass and dog bowl water, then made a quick call to an emergency window replacement company. The window company sent a man out that morning.

When he arrived, we both stood by the broken window as I regaled him with the story of what happened. I said I had never seen a hawk that close up before and did not know why it had crashed through my kitchen window. I assumed it had flown low and thought it was entering a cave, a miscalculation made worse because it did not see the glass window in the way.

The window replacement man—an old country local—looked wryly among the debris below the window sill and picked up our Italian Alessi rabbit toothpick holder that usually lived by the kitchen window. The Alessi design for the plastic rabbit exaggerated the ears. "That hawk," he said, "was after your young rabbit here."

"But," I said, "that's a very small rabbit to see from way up in the sky."

The man just shrugged and advised that I find another, more internal location for the toothpick holder, or he was sure the hawk would be back sooner than I might like.

Despite our everyday sense of isolation and seclusion in the valley, we were always being watched, even if only by the local animals. We lived in a place that belonged to many creatures. Most went about their own business and stayed out of our way. But others kept watch over us because our territory *was* their business, their livelihood, and their home. That hawk hunted field mice and small rabbits. Its job was to notice anything different or anything that moved in that territory, including us. Furthermore, it had learned which mental shapes meant food. And two rabbit ears inside a recently built cave entrance fit the bill. We moved the toothpick holder.

Often we think we are alone, and even if we think we are alone geographically, we mostly are not. Being alone is more of a feeling than an actuality. As the medievalist Ben Morgan argues, we have not been in origin, nor in development, nor in an everyday sense alone.[1] Born from a mother and raised dependent on others, the presence of our self is an intertwined existence by definition. When we sit in a public place, others—here and there, from time to time, for shorter or longer periods—notice us, even if they do not directly engage with us. If this were not mostly the case, pickpockets would not need clandestine techniques to avoid eye contact. Only in rooms with drawn curtains do we achieve the privacy we need to do private things. But in normal and usual life, no matter how we personally feel, we are seen, even closely watched.

This is true, and it is an aspiration for most cultures. This particular type of a remote social connectivity—of watching conduct—is emphasized in all the holy books of our own modern cultures, though we might not think of them much when we read them only occasionally.

> The Lord will watch over your coming and going both now and forevermore. (Ps. 121:8)

> For He will command His angels concerning you to guard you in all your ways. (Ps. 91:11–12)

> And let us watch out for one another to provoke love and good works. (Heb. 10:24)

> For every soul there is a guardian watching over it. (Koran 86:11)

A Pattern Directing the Patterns

The idea that we are being watched over, even from what may seem to be great distances—by the gods, the angels, by each other, or by an unknown guardian—is old and deep and culturally universal. It has always had a mostly benevolent meaning. Watching over another has simultaneously meant that something precious is at the center of one's watchful eye—you are valuable to someone somewhere, however close, however far. Antoine de Saint-Exupéry describes it beautifully in a passage from his story *The Little Prince*:

> To be sure, an ordinary passerby would think that my rose looked just like you—the rose that belongs to me. But in herself alone she is more important than all the hundreds of you other roses: because it is she that I have watered; because it is she that I have put under the glass globe; because it is she that I have sheltered behind the screen; because it is for her that I have killed the caterpillars (except the two or three that we saved to become butterflies); because it is she that I have listened to, when she grumbled, or boasted, or even sometimes when she said nothing. Because she is my rose . . . it is the time you have wasted for your rose that makes your rose so important.[2]
>
>   "Men have forgotten this truth," said the fox. "But you must not forget it. You become responsible, forever, for what you have tamed. You are responsible for your rose."

You can imagine the hawk from my story telling it this way, can you not? The hawk would speak not about a rose but the little valley where we lived for a while. It is *his* valley, not just any valley at all but the valley that he has fed from and watched over for many years. That valley was precious to that hawk for reasons perfectly in tune with the biological needs of his station in the food chain. But for whatever biological reasons may drive its instinct for mice and small rabbits, whatever competition it has won to monopolize that particular valley, the end result is the creation and maintenance of a *value*—a precious value—for that bird. And the hawk jealously watches over it.

Humans are the same. Not only does watching over someone indicate a precious value to the one who watches, but it is also a precious value to be watched over. Think of the many love songs that sing the praises of being the center of another's caring gaze and attentions. As Ira and George Gershwin famously described it,

There's a somebody I'm longing to see.
I hope that he turns out to be
Someone who'll watch over me.

In circumstances of dying, death, and bereavement, we see this watching-over behavior greatly intensify and focus. More commonly we call it *vigilance*. We hold vigils by the sickbeds of our loved ones in hospitals, intensive care units, and hospices, or later still at their funerals, and even at cemeteries. Many cemeteries, for example, attract more visitors than popular tourist sites.[3] And most who go to cemeteries do not go for the spooky thrills; they go to visit their loved ones, even in death. Such watchful behavior is merely an extension of the watchfulness—in the spirit of loving care—that most of us show elsewhere in our lives: our attendance at school plays, graduations, award nights, weddings, baptisms and bar mitzvahs, and so on. These are the ways that—often taken for granted, and therefore so often overlooked—we watch over one another. We keep vigil for the ones precious to us.

VIGILS ARE NORMALLY associated with attendance by family and friends to one who is sick or dying. It is sometimes thought that these are old practices associated with traditional village life, or that *vigil* is an archaic word that no longer applies to the behavior during visiting hours in hospitals or intensive care units. This is not true. *Vigil* not only describes the loyal attendance to those incapacitated by serious illness but also describes what usually happens among the seriously ill, the attendees, and those outside that support circle, like the doctors, nurses, and priests.

A vigil for the dying, also sometimes known as a deathwatch, is a widely observed social phenomenon.[4] In some nursing homes, nursing staff are allocated to a resident who is close to death to monitor any complications or unexpected medical difficulties in the resident's final hours and to ensure that he or she does not die alone.[5] In intensive care units, where some patients face an expected death, close family and friends commonly hold vigils in the final hours.[6] Because dying is carefully monitored, hospice care units also attract family vigils for the dying.[7] All of these vigils in institutional settings can be viewed as extensions of the vigils for the dying at home.[8]

Much of the behavior commonly observed around vigils for the dying is derivative—in other words, it emanates from past traditional behavior seen more commonly in wakes. Although the traditional wake is receding all over the world, some social behaviors have remained in the bedside circumstances of modern dying. Vigils for the dying consist of small groups of family and friends assembling by the bedside of a seriously ill relative in the terminal stages of dying. Health-care professionals, commonly doctors, nurses, or nursing home caregivers, usually determine the commencement of dying. They then notify close relatives, and family and friends come together at the bedside of the dying relative. This intimate support group of the dying person usually stays by the bedside until death occurs.[9]

The palliative researchers Sinead Donnelly and C. N. Donnelly observed that, at least in hospice care units, vigils for the dying can include between six and fourteen relatives.[10] It is common in vigils for relatives to hold hands with the dying person, to reminisce with him or her (even if the person is unconscious), and to offer him or her food and drink. It is usually described as a "very private" or "family" experience.[11] In contemporary Ireland, for example, Donnelly and Donnelly observed that the previously described conduct may be supplemented by prayers, candles, laughing, crying, and the exchange of family stories.[12]

Occasionally, a hospice care service may supplement these family activities with the provision of music during the deathwatch.[13] Trudy Read and Judith Wuest observe that vigils are times of "protective watchfulness," and this commonly extends into the time after death and before burial—a conduct and period more usually identified with the traditional wake.[14] In order to participate in the vigil, family and friends often arrange for bereavement leave from employers and make travel and accommodation arrangements. Often different tasks and responsibilities for the vigil are divided into specific roles for family members and friends—spokesperson, principal visitor, principal caregiver, informant, chief communicator with doctors, and so on.[15] It is also important to note that whether the dying person is conscious or not, he or she is "part" of this vigil of watchfulness and activity.[16]

Although descriptions of vigils for the dying person often emphasize the importance of other people's watchfulness, they often overlook that the dying person also participates. The chaplain Andrew Edmeads reminds us of Christ's request in the Garden of Gethsemane to "watch with me" as he faces his arrest, conviction, and death.[17] This idea of "watching" oneself die occurs in many first-person accounts of dying[18] and several famous literary accounts from old fiction, like Leo Tolstoy's *The Death of Ivan Illyich*.[19] We even see it in recent nonfiction—for example, Mitch Albom's *Tuesdays with Morrie*.[20]

The presence of vigils for the dying in modern health-care settings may in part be explained by how dying has become prolonged and highly personalized.[21] Coming together, for example, creates an obvious social recognition of a prospective loss that simultaneously provides support to dying persons and their immediate circle of intimates.

The modern presence of the vigil for the dying is neither new nor confined to functions about loss, support, or being together. Vigils for the dying are persistent and remnant traditions of the wake. In etymological terms, the words *vigil* and *wake* are part of a cognate group that commonly refer to each other.[22] The pattern of social behavior seems to do more than merely provide mutual identification with grief and personal support. The significance of this "watching over" behavior is often more practical than merely symbolic of coming together out of some notion of social solidarity.

The American anthropologist Victor Turner argued that within a transition process between serious illness and death—or serious illness and recovery—both the ill and the attendees become what he calls "threshold people."[23] Their position in the social world of the living is stripped. They are purged of their former status. According to Turner, people in this liminal time, this transition period, have an absence of their usual status and are reduced to humility rather than pride of position.[24] They must accept pain, suffering, and other ordeals as part of their transition and must submit to a greater authority. These are the common characteristics of living people who are imminently dying and those who are attending the dying. Liminal states shatter norms and create emotional chaos and confusion—joy, sorrow, love, anger, resentment, guilt, fear—in wakes for the dead and vigils for the dying.

Roger Grainger argues that such turmoil creates the impression of a "perilous journey," one that demands support such as rallying around the bedside of the dying or, later, providing company, weapons, food, and so on in the graves of those departed and departing.[25]

Some of the social purposes of sitting with the dead also apply to sitting with the seriously ill or dying loved one. These purposes are the following:

1. Ensuring that death has taken place (also called a deathwatch).
2. Protecting the seriously ill or dead from harm or other hazards. In traditional societies this might be "evil spirits" visiting the deathbed. In modern times, this might equally

apply to poor nursing or medical care, professional neglect, disturbing noises, and premature lamentations that might prolong dying; it also includes ensuring minute-by-minute care in the final hours.[26]

3. Providing social support and placating the departing person on his or her onward journey. This is particularly relevant when the ill or dying person is conscious. Vigils provide encouragement, support, conversation, humor, reminiscence, and practical help with eating or drinking.

4. Soothing the inner turmoil of the dying. Here friends and family provide social support to the ill and dying and attend to their psychology—their anxiety, worries, even panic, and bodily sufferings. Vigils also function to support the supporters, bolstering them against their own experiences of grief and anguish. Grief and loss do not begin at funerals or death but well before, during the course of the last illness.

5. Expressing dissent and resistance to new forms of civil or clerical control. A less well known and circulated idea, the idea of the wake as a form of social criticism and resistance has been discussed by many writers.[27] They describe the distaste and open opposition of church authorities to the traditional wake. In Britain and Ireland, for example, the alcoholic excesses, the satirizing of clergy, and occasional sexual promiscuity so common in wakes have produced long-standing disapproval from the church. Wakes, as long-standing traditions, often owed their origins to early pagan ceremony and commemoration[28] and represented one of the few traditional vestiges of pre-Christian values and authority.

Modern versions of these forms of social resistance may be seen in the tensions between health-care staff and family. Sometimes conflicts arise over the adequacy of food or drink or the desire of nursing staff to continue care of potential pressure sore areas, even when patients are near death. Family and nursing staff may have different agendas in their care of the dying person. Vigils for the dying can be ways for friends and family to reclaim both the space and control over the dying person and his or her needs. This can disturb hospital routines. Communication between family and health-care staff can be a particular problem in hospitals and nursing home care settings where routines and social protocols for the care of dying patients may not be well established, or when these institutions have no set protocols for assisting stressed and grieving families dealing with their loved ones at the end of life.[29]

Vigils for the dying—as early stages of the traditional wake—are social rites that do more than simply manage the emotional turmoil of mutual loss between the dying person and his or her intimates. They also provide their participants with more than opportunities for saying goodbye and companionship. Vigils, like wakes, demonstrate a set of purposes that encourage participants to protect, advocate, and support the journeys of illness and dying with the nonclinical, cultural equipment of everyday life—food, drink, laughter, storytelling, and sometimes religious ritual and practices. These comfort the dying in an event widely viewed—even among secular populations—as mysterious, if not mystical. These are long-standing assumptions and practices, and they encourage and support families and friends to believe that the common currency of their everyday lives—social and spiritual support for each other—has real value, even in the valley of the shadow of death.

Underlaying and energizing these social purposes in keeping vigil are the facts of human attachment. We keep vigil because we view our relationship to the one who is seriously ill as precious. Love draws us to the other. We watch over them, hope they do not go, but if they do leave us, we want to be there to bid farewell, to offer our companionship at the end. We offer our gifts to the dying in the context of a joint journey of watchfulness. This is the vigil we keep at the end of life for each other. And these are the exact same motivations of the dead toward us as living but dying beings.

WHEN YOU VISIT your loved one in a hospital or hospice, you follow a set protocol: you go in, greet the person verbally or with a kiss, hand over a gift of flowers or candy or a greeting card, sit for a while and talk, and leave. Or, if the patient is unconscious, you might stay until there is a change that signals recovery, or until death. You might stay until the patient becomes conscious. If the patient is unconscious, you may still talk, and you may hold their hand. The patient does not always remember those acts upon recovery, but sometimes they do. But you do this less for the sake that they might remember than the fact that you want to keep watch over them.

If the dead were in your place, and you were seriously ill, dying, or grieving, what behavior might you expect from them? It should come as no anthropological surprise that the logic of visitation by the dead should follow the logic of the living where a dying loved one is concerned. If that is true, when the dead visit their loved ones, they express themselves through the same social protocol: greet verbally or with a kiss, hand over a gift, talk, stay a while, come and go.

In the examples of deathbed visions (DBVs), then, should there be any wonder why the dead visit in these circumstances? They visit because they are close relatives and friends. Whether these relationships emerge from the afterlife or merely from the mind of the dying person is, again, irrelevant. What matters here is the sense of this, the meaning inherent in the appearances themselves. And that sense has an obvious precedent in our own and immediate conduct at the bedside of our seriously ill and dying.

We do not know who the beings of light are, but we do know—to continue the logic of our anthropological review of the situation—that the deathbed is not solely populated by friends and family. There *are* other beings present with us as living people, usually these are health-care professionals such as doctors, nurses, chaplains, and counselors. Sometimes, there are people rarely seen but who have a connection with the dying person—a lawyer, an old business partner, a "distant friend" who was really an old lover not known to any family member. We have already discussed the possible role of beings of light as not in the category of friends and relatives but more like emergency social services personnel. If there are "care professionals" on the life side of the deathbed, then why should it be unusual to identify similar personnel on the death side of the deathbed?

The social logic must be followed by the visitors, and that logic will be a mirror of social relationships and customs as we know them. If a large octopus wearing blue jeans appeared in the chair beside the deathbed and attempted to sell the person home insurance, this would be an obvious source of stress for the dying person and the supporters who hear about it later. It would not make sense.

On the other hand, the dead are known, they explain themselves, they reassure in the customary way, and the reason for their visit—like the reason for your visit—is known and makes sense to the dying person. If we keep vigil, why not them?

In near-death experiences (NDEs), the victim of the car crash, the person who collapses with a heart attack, or the victim who almost drowns experiences a sensation of company. At first this sensation may not be clear. An out-of-body experience or sensation of traveling through darkness may precede any sensation of company. But then soon, the dying person will see a light. If the person proceeds further into the experience, beings will inevitably appear. In some cases the beings will appear quite suddenly and early—during an out-of-body experience, for example. But when they appear, they will relate to the person as though he or she is a precious thing to them—because they are family or friends, or because the person has just been ushered into a social services being of light who makes it very clear that he or she is precious and loved.

We have only the reports of those who survive. At some point during the experience, it turns out to be an administrative error and the person must return to his or her former life on earth. Sometimes, a choice is offered, to return or to stay.

It is rare indeed that the person who is near death reports no one at all, that when he or she was in "another space," no one came. It is not unheard of, and we do not know why this happens, but for the majority of cases, someone is waiting for the person. In other words, they appear to have prepared for this. Doesn't this imply they have been observing? In fact, that they have been watching for some time?

For the bereaved, who are not usually dying, and who are often going about their daily business, the dead also visit and often say or imply that they know what is going on in the lives of those they are clearly watching over. Sometimes, like the appearance of Heather to me, or the appearance of my piano teacher's dead mother, there is not a strong suggestion of a watching brief (that is, there is no obvious sense that the dead were constantly watching a person before their later sudden appearance to them). However, a moment's thought suggests otherwise. The nature of Heather's message to me was in context. Heather knew where I was, what I was doing there at the motel, why I was there, and what my friend Jake was feeling and offered her messages to me in a context of which she was thoroughly appraised.

Although subtler than Heather's insertion into my situation, my piano teacher's mother chose her moment and site to appear. She did not appear when my piano teacher was playing the piano or watching television or washing the dishes. She chose to appear at a quiet time, when my piano teacher was least distracted. She chose a place on the sofa in full view of the kitchen door, just when my piano teacher emerged with her orange and paring knife. This has all the hallmarks of a set piece. This was a deliberate act suggesting prior surveillance and planning. I suggest here that this style of obvious surveillance conduct is best understood as someone keeping a close eye on us, of a vigil being kept.

Vigils by the Dead

Let us remind ourselves of the multiple reasons we keep vigils for those we love whose lives are imperiled: to ensure that death (or recovery) has actually taken place; to protect the departing soul from evil spirits (mainly applies to people with traditional beliefs); to provide support and placate the departing soul on his or her journey; to soothe the inner turmoil for the dying and his or her supporters; and to resist new forms of civil or clerical control.

On the other hand, vigils for the dying (DBVs and NDEs) by the dead may have the following similar reasons, clearly derivative of the concerns that most of us would or do have when attending our own dying people. These reasons from the already-dead person's point of view are the following:

1. To ensure that death occurs expeditiously or is given a guided return. This refers to the welcoming-party aspect of DBVs and NDEs. Greetings and advice may occur here.
2. To protect the departing person from any transitional problems. Dying people may find the transition particularly difficult or traumatic, or there may be hazards in the other place or within the mind of the dying person. Re-orientation or transformations may occur here.
3. To provide support and placate the departing soul on his or her journey. Gifts may be offered here.
4. To soothe the inner turmoil for the dying and his or her supporters. Gifts may also be offered here.

For vigils by the dead that might watch over the bereaved, these purposes appear to be consistent with those we have seen by the

Vigils

living for their dead, and the dead watching over their living who happen to be dying. These reasons are the following:

1. To assert their continuing presence within a previous relationship. The appearance to the bereaved is similar to our own appearance for the living who are dying. Although many dying people will be insensible to our presence, some will not; and for those for whom contact is possible, the bereavement vision is a prompt and a reminder of the ongoing existence and importance of their relationship—as all vigils are. Greetings or simple continuance may occur here.
2. To support and encourage the bereaved to continue their journey. As part of the continuing relationship, the purposes of all loving relationships continue to be served. This means that advice and direction may occur here.
3. To soothe the inner turmoil of the bereaved and their supporters. Reorientation and transformation may occur here as prime motivation for the visit or as an aftereffect.
4. To resolve mutual needs and expectations for either party. Gifts may be offered here.

The one outstanding reason for keeping vigil for the dying—to express dissent and resist new forms of civil or clerical control—seems absent from the watching conduct by the dead. Or is it? The one interesting fact that emerges from the worldwide prevalence figures of DBVs, NDEs, and visions of the bereaved is the strength of those estimates despite ever-increasing secularization.

It is not simply that more and more people are no longer churchgoers or religious, but also that there are increasing challenges to the idea of the sacred, the mystical, and the spiritual. In the industrial and affluent nations of the West, there is less a battle between science and religion and more a mutual ignoring of each other. There remains a certain minimal level of dialogue and debate, and we can see this in the academic controversies between evolutionary scientists and creationist advocates, or between religionists and humanists in abortion or euthanasia policy debates. But mostly people compartmentalize their often parallel sentiments—using their smartphones to read their daily horoscope, for example.

In a smart world, a technological world, a progressively materialist world where people nevertheless hedge their bets, mystical experiences near death are not only a bit of a civic embarrassment but also a criticism against our arrogance in the modern world. The images that come to us from these NDEs, and the light beings that emerge from them, are not prescribed in most world religions, despite the occasional near-death report of these beings in specifically doctrinal terms. We can assume, at least in terms of our current politics of knowledge, that the watchful gaze that the dead keep on our affairs, as evidenced in our dreams and waking experiences while dying or grieving, are indeed proof of a fifth and final purpose to their mysterious vigils. And that is to dissent and resist new forms of civil or clerical control. Visits to us by our dead buck the very system that argues these visits are impossible.

TO END where we began in this chapter, what became of the young collie? Her name was Pop, and she was the last of our three collies to die. Pop was particularly fond of and close to Minty, the collie who died before her. Pop never quite seemed to get over Minty's death. She grieved for her friend. She often cut a lonely figure after that, and she seemed to quickly grow old and fragile, chronically ill with one ailment or another.

Some years after we had left the rural property in Australia and were living in a village in England, I watched over her in the days before her eventual death from bladder cancer. On what I knew would be the final day, I took the day off from work to be with her. In the early morning, I took her out to the back garden to toilet. She could just barely walk.

But then suddenly her ears pricked up. She looked across the back lawn and started barking with glee. Pop always had a particular joyous bark saved for greetings. Suddenly she shot off into the backyard. She skipped and bounced around like a rocking horse, the way she did when she was happy. Pop was trailing some invisible thing around in circles. It was about her height, judging from her gaze. Then just as suddenly she broke away, following it toward the house. Then, she turned away again and headed up toward the front lawn. Her eyes were fixed on it, and I could see she was delighted with her new company. This was an old dog dying of cancer, in the terminal stage, who could barely walk or stay upright for the last forty-eight hours.

It was early in the morning, so I had to stop her from barking or risk the neighbor's wrath. But I had to catch her first. Eventually I got a hold of her, and I lifted her into my arms and carried her into the house. In the house, she looked at me in a disappointed way and eventually lay down in her usual sickbed position. After that she could not stand at all, and she died some twelve hours later.

What did she see? I saw nothing, and she could not tell me anything. But I knew her, and I could tell that whatever she saw, she recognized it, took delight in it, and played a last game with it. Whatever it was, it seemed to be a gift to her. And from what we now know, I would not be surprised if she made plans to repay it the very next morning.

Conclusion

NOT EVERYONE GETS a visit from their dead. When I speak about this topic I am often asked, especially from the recently bereaved, why they have not been visited by their dead. If the prevalence of visits from the dead is so high—one in three people—why have they missed out?

My friend Jake asked me the same question when I told him I thought his wife had visited me one evening, even while I was in his company. People rarely ask this question in an academic kind of way. They are usually desperate for contact; even after many years they cannot quench the yearning for the one they have lost. That is, after all, what grief is like.

And when I speak about gifts or the vigils that the dead maintain over us, just as we maintain vigils for our own dying, these terms make some listeners, and some readers here, feel even more like they have missed out, been overlooked, forgotten. That will often hurt more, feel more like rejection. That too is entirely understandable. But if you are one of these people, and you have read this book up to here, then I must remind you again what it is we

Conclusion

are doing in all of these discussions, before weighing some possible explanations.

First of all, as I described in the preface, this is not a book extolling the possibilities of personal survival over death. The purpose of this book is to identify the meaning behind a social phenomenon—why our dead and their being-of-light friends come to us in the way that they do. I have argued that, whether these come from somewhere else or from within our own minds, the dead and their friends must approach us with the behavior and motivations that are characteristic of them in life. If they did not, we simply would not recognize them and would find new contact with them frightening or threatening.

This is not a crude argument about cultural reproduction, recycling the view that what we see is purely a function of what we expect to see, because that is not true. Rather, when there are new or novel experiences, those experiences and our understanding of them must share a common social language to make sense to us. This is the key to all effective communication and applies to all situations we expect and those we do not expect. This grammar of everyday life—our usual understandings of things like greeting behavior, personal change, rites of passage, gift exchange, or vigil conduct—helps us negotiate all our interpersonal experience, and that must include experiences between ourselves and the dead and supernatural-like beings.

If you accept this anthropological insight as true, even self-evidently true, then what is true for sightings of the dead must also be true for nonsightings of the dead. We cannot cherry-pick. For those who have not had visits from their dead but would like to, this is possibly a more bitter pill to swallow than for those who have seen their dead. But that difference in reception does not alter the sociological facts. And the facts seem to be that within all social life there is remarkable variation in a single experience.

I am always amazed when I meet people who have not seen even a single *Star Wars* film. But it is often for the most ordinary reasons.

They likely do not have children, do not like science fiction films (and there are a lot of these people in the world), or do not live near a movie theater or own a television or a computer. Yes, there are still people in the world without these technologies, millions of them. The world is not America or France or Japan. And a lot of people do not speak English, apparently the only language used by both the Empire and the Rebels. We often forget this, so submerged are we in our own affluence and ethnocentrism.

Not everyone has been visited by Mormons either. People are frequently surprised when I make this observation. And it is not for want of Mormon motivation. I am sure they would like to visit every front door they could. But alas, there are just not enough Mormons in the world. It has less to do with the curb appeal of your house or the crying need of your soul, and more to do with being short-staffed. In any case, you may have been out every time they came—at work, in the back garden, at the golf course, in the bathroom singing so loudly you did not hear the doorbell. It is not always about you (as a person). Sometimes circumstances conspire to exclude you.

Remember, too, that there are also important perceptual considerations to entertain. Recall the insights and arguments of chapter 3. Let me quote an important reminder from the section that speaks to the psychology of perception that must prioritize by rules about what is and what is not important to notice:

> If these objects are slightly altered, the mind tends to distort them to make them fit into the rules. The result is a distortion of the image. This is why many people simply cannot see things unless they are shown how. Many people's perception routine simply deletes images that are before them but unacceptable to their own rules about what to see.

Most people are not tuned in to see dead people. That is normal. In Japan, up to 90 percent of the bereaved will report visits from

Conclusion

their dead as either a sensed presence or a voice or a full-blown apparition.[1] But at the same time, it is normal for Japanese people to interact with their dead. This is a key reason they have a *butsodan* (a small altar for offerings and where conversation can be had with the dead) in their houses. It is also why they celebrate the festival of *o-bon*, where the dead are invited home for a couple of days as an annual courtesy.

People who have these kinds of rituals and cultural ideas have perceptual rules that are more receptive to contact with the deceased. We are not talking about being more likely to create or imagine that contact, but—from whatever source that contact may emanate—they are more likely to be receptive to the sights, sounds, or feelings that contact makes when it does come. For others in the West, it is just as important to realize that many, perhaps even most, people who are bereaved do not receive contact. A 30 percent or 50 percent prevalence of bereavement visions is not a 100 percent prevalence. So what separates the haves from the have-nots? The epidemiological answer is, we do not know.

I would like to tell you that atheists and skeptics never see their dead, but that is not true. I would also like to say that those who believe in life after death are more likely to see their dead, but neither is that true. Some have argued that those who grieve "hard"—who are obsessional in their grieving—may be less likely to report seeing their dead. We have no evidence that is true either.

Recall the case of Katherine Russell Rich, who, in the midst of drunken despair about her life and her serious breast cancer, in the middle of all this emotional chaos, is visited by a violet-colored light that brings her comfort. Why? We do not know. The religious studies scholar Carl Becker, who has conducted significant work on mystical near-death experiences, is often asked by people why their dead do not visit. He has a simple question for them: Are you sure they haven't? Like the unsuccessful first-timers failing to solve a Magic Eye puzzle, those who have not seen their dead are urged to look again.[2]

It is also important to remind ourselves of the problems we have when we keep vigil over those whose lives are in medical crisis. Ask yourself if the following might apply to your own possible insensibilities:

> When you visit your loved one in a hospital or hospice, you follow a set protocol: you go in, greet the person verbally or with a kiss, hand over a gift of flowers or candy or a greeting card, sit for a while and talk, and leave. Or, if the patient is unconscious, you might stay until there is a change that signals recovery, or until death. You might stay until the patient becomes conscious. If the patient is unconscious, you may still talk, and you may hold their hand. The patient does not always remember those acts upon recovery, but sometimes they do. But you do this less for the sake that they might remember than the fact that you want to keep watch over them.
>
> If the dead were in your place, and you were seriously ill, dying, or grieving, what behavior might you expect from them? It should come as no anthropological surprise that the logic of visitation by the dead should follow the logic of the living where a dying loved one is concerned. If that is true, when the dead visit their loved ones, they express themselves through the same social protocol: greet verbally or with a kiss, hand over a gift, talk, stay a while, come and go. *If it is serious, the dead might stay until you become conscious of them. If you are not conscious of the dead, they may still bring a gift and they may talk, but you do not always remember these acts upon recovery, but sometimes you do. And when you do, you may report it as a "dream" about the dead or as a waking experience of the dead visiting.*

Here we are crucially reminded that even when we keep vigil over the living who are dying, those loved ones may not perceive or even later remember our presence. Why, then, is it so difficult to see these matters in reverse—the vigil in the mirror. Sometimes we are "un-

Conclusion

conscious" to this type of contact. We are determinedly focused on things in our everyday world and our worries therein. However, this does not mean the dead do not see us or do not visit us, because maybe we simply do not see them for reasons best understood within our own psychological makeup. And not seeing them now does not mean we will not see them in the future.

When a friend of mine in the Australian countryside used to boast that he had never hit a kangaroo in all the years he drove to his country property, that boasting lasted only until he finally hit one. It just took a little longer in his case. In that part of the country, it was merely a matter of time. But he thought he was a living miracle. Turns out he was just luckier than most. Not yet does not mean never. Or to put this in existential terms, both the possibilities of surprises and the hopes that reside patiently within them remain on the table.

When all is said and done, there is a possibility that it might, in fact, be about you after all—or rather about your relationship with your deceased. There is much we do not know, even in all our case studies about the relationship between ourselves as living individuals and what happens to that relationship when one of us dies.

The near-death experience, the deathbed vision, and the visions encountered by bereaved people are not sudden events without context. There is always a context that provides the meaning. The problem is that when people tell their stories, they often hold back that context from the listener or have that context edited out by those with greater interest in the mystical bits. Some people can never disclose the backstory of their relationship with the deceased—it is simply too private a matter. And it can be a highly delicate ethical matter to pry. If Katherine Russell Rich simply declared that she was home one evening having a drink, and then *bang!* a being of light entered the room for no reason at all, we would take away a very different impression from her real story. And many stories are told like this. But do we really know if this is the real context of the encounter? The backstory of Katherine's long fight with breast cancer—and with despair, social rejection, work discrimination, and isolation—makes sense of the visit for us, and probably for Katherine too.

The sociological implication that this suggests for some of those who claim not to receive visits from their dead is perhaps the same. To explain why there has been no visit without understanding the relationship between the yearned-for and the yearner is potentially futile. Everyone knows that relationships are complex and there may be good reasons why you have not seen them, but that does not mean they are not visiting. Conversely, there may be good reasons that make you capable of "seeing" but equally good reasons for them not to choose to visit. And I hasten to add, *those reasons do not have to be negative*; there may be positive reasons why you cannot see or they cannot visit. I merely make the point that politics in relationships may be a factor in nonvisitation. Because that is the way it is in life, and the history of anthropology concerning relationships between the dead and the living suggests that those relationships play by the same rules.

In summary, then, we can say you have not been visited for a few reasons. Perhaps they have visited but you have not noticed. Or they have not visited for their own reasons and they are not sharing at the moment. Or the circumstances, for reasons we do not understand, are not right. Or there is a context to your relationship that might complicate contact for either side. Or they will, just not yet. Be patient.

You can see that there is much research to do.[3] The bulk of our academic energies seems to go into torturing our current data until it morphs into evidence for life after death or supports a novel kind of hallucination. Very little effort goes into linking personal experiences with social determinants of contact—in other words, attempting to determine how these kinds of personal experiences are understood in the context of one's biography, and how different patterns of biographical storyline might predict contact. To what extent are these biographical narratives shaped by the broader cultural scripts of the wider society, and to what extent do they depart from them? Which parts of a personal narrative reflect, and which parts are critical of the dominant mores and discourses of the day? How do we incorporate unusual experiences like those described in this book into the fabric of our usual social logic, our values, and our lifestyles? And what effect does that have on us as individuals?

Visits from our dead are important. They are not to be classed together with Ouija board games, horror films, and palm readings at the flea market. Visits from the dead are widespread and have always been widespread. Their prevalence figures eclipse figures for worldwide prevalence of color blindness or mental illness. Visits from the dead and their being-of-light friends are transcultural.

The cultural scripts from religion and science often fail us here simply because they debate merely the source and not the meaning of these experiences for those who encounter them. The helping professions can be more helpful if they join forces with the social sciences—history, anthropology, folk studies, and sociology—to forge an understanding of how these experiences change us. Visits from our dead usually mean us well. Their effects are overwhelmingly positive. These experiences are not pathologies to be treated. They are extensions of our experiences of love and loss that must be integrated into our personal and social lives. It is up to us to help that integration.

Visits from the dead are potentially powerful sources of personal stability, social connectivity, and emotional resilience. Recognizing this will restore this core collection of previously hidden, interpersonal experiences to our sense of normality. For in these personal matters, what is no longer hidden is no longer feared.

Acknowledgments

I WOULD LIKE TO BEGIN my brief list of thanks and acknowledgments by recognizing Stephen Wesley, my publisher at Columbia University Press, who, over dinner and possibly one too many glasses of wine, suggested I write a book like this. At that time I had just delivered my last volume to him, *The Inner Life of the Dying Person*. That book contains a short section dealing with transformative near-death experiences, which, during our long dinner in a New York diner, he encouraged me to elaborate in greater detail. Stephen was fascinated by the comings and goings of our dead and surprised by the other "beings" that also came and went, sometimes accompanying our dead, sometimes not. He suggested that there was a need for a book that avoided the crazy debates about hallucinations versus heaven. We both believed that there must be large numbers of people curious to understand their own and others' "visitation" experiences. Stephen thought that these audiences might appreciate a book that attempts to help them with this, since this is a topic that remains difficult to discuss openly in

Acknowledgments

public. He suggested it. Here it is, Stephen. Sorry there are no "blue monkeys" in it. No more wine for you!

Most of my research, and therefore most of the books I have written during my career, has been in the study of the conduct of dying and the development of public health models for its care. I have long been interested in all forms of dying, not simply through terminal illness, and not merely in contemporary circumstances either. My work has examined the dying experience up to twelve months before death as well as much closer, in the final days and hours. I have contributed to debates about the determination of death as well as the best ways to design hospice and palliative care services. I have been one of the founding advocates of civic engagement and participation in end-of-life care. And because I cover all these quite different areas inside the tall shadow of death, I occasionally examine mystical experiences near death too. It is part of the job.

When I do cover this heavily misunderstood topic, only two things ever seem to happen. The work is completely ignored, because I am not contributing to one of the two rather meager discourses that are deemed acceptable in this field, or I get criticized for *appearing* not to join one of them. Ergo, I am a "closet" skeptic, or I am a "closet" believer in the afterlife. Or perhaps a sneaky academic who wants it both ways. Sorry, guys, I am neither. You need to get out more. I am from the social sciences. There is more to understanding daily life than chemistry or chakras! Come and see us sometime. In the meantime, I thank my academic colleague and wife, Jan Fook, for her continuous feedback on my work. She, along with many of my colleagues from sociology, anthropology, folklore studies, religious studies, and clinical medicine, understands the social value of meaning-making for clinical encounters, interpersonal relationships, and community life more broadly. The support of my colleagues has always been crucial to me as a writer, keeping me focused on both the promise and the benefits of the social sciences for our communities.

Acknowledgments

I also wish to acknowledge the support of the University of Minnesota, Morris, which awarded me a Distinguished Visiting Professor in the Liberal Arts post in 2018. This post gave me the opportunity to teach as well as deliver a couple of public lectures to try out some of the ideas in this book with students, faculty, and the local community. I was also able to complete this book during that time. I am grateful to my home university, the University of Bradford in the United Kingdom, for allowing me to take time out of my usual duties to avail myself of this wonderful opportunity. Thanks are also due to George Millington, who provided valuable research assistance in the early stages of this book.

I have drawn from previously published work as part of the writing for this book. I acknowledge, with thanks, various excerpts drawn from my previous work: A. Kellehear, "Joy," from *Eternity and Me: The Everlasting Things in Life and Death* (Melbourne: Hill of Content, 2000; U.S. edition, New York: Routledge, 2004), 46–49; A. Kellehear, "Unusual Perceptions at the End of Life: Limitations to the Diagnosis of Hallucinations in Palliative Medicine," *BMJ Supportive and Palliative Care* 7, no. 3 (2017): 238–246; and A. Kellehear, "Vigils for the Dying: Origin and Functions of a Persistent Tradition," *Illness, Crisis & Loss* 21, no. 2 (2013): 109–124.

Finally, I would like to acknowledge with thanks the various acquaintances, friends, and colleagues whose names have been changed here but who are part of some of the stories that I retell. You know who you are. My thanks are also due to Pop, who gave me two wonderful stories to retell here. Your stories, like all my memories of you, will remain with me forever.

Notes

Preface

1. S. P. Muthumana, M. Kumari, A. Kellehear, S. Kumar, and F. Moosa, "Deathbed Visions from India: A Study of Family Observations in Northern Kerala," *Omega: Journal of Death & Dying* 62, no. 2 (2010): 95–107.
2. A. Kellehear, V. Pogonet, R. Mindruta-Stratan, and V. Gorelco, *Care of the Dying in the Republic of Moldova* (Chisinau, Moldova: UNESCO, 2011).
3. A. Kellehear, V. Pogonet, R. Mindruta-Stratan, and V. Gorelco, "Deathbed Visions from the Republic of Moldova: A Content Analysis of Family Observations." *Omega: Journal of Death & Dying* 64, no. 4 (2011–2012): 310.
4. Kellehear et al., "Deathbed Visions from the Republic of Moldova," 311.
5. B. Guggenheim and J. Guggenheim, *Hello from Heaven* (New York: Bantam, 1996), 92.
6. Guggenheim and Guggenheim, *Hello from Heaven*, 92.
7. R. Blanes and D. E. Santo, eds., *The Social Life of Spirits* (Chicago: University of Chicago Press, 2014).

1. Visitors Near Death

1. W. Barrett, *Deathbed Visions* (1926; repr., Wellingborough, UK: Aquarian Press, 1989), 68–69.

1. Visitors Near Death

2. S. P. Muthumana, M. Kumari, A. Kellehear, F. Kumar, and F. Moosa, "Deathbed Visions from India: A Study of Family Observations in Northern Kerala," *Omega: Journal of Death & Dying* 62, no. 2 (2010–2011): 97–109.

3. Muthumana et al., "Deathbed Visions from India," 105.

4. S. Blackmore, *Dying to Live: Science and the Near-Death Experience* (London: Grafton, 1993).

5. For the reasoning behind my use of the phrase "visions of the bereaved," please see chapter 2, note 37.

6. For example, see J. Hicks, *Death and Eternal Life* (London: Collins, 1976).

7. I. Wilson, *The After Death Experience* (New York: Sidgwick & Jackson, 1987), 147.

8. Wilson, *The After Death Experience*, 149.

9. B. Elder, *And When I Die, Will I Be Dead?* (Sydney: ABC Books, 1987).

10. Elder, *And When I Die, Will I Be Dead?*, 21–22.

11. M. Morse with P. Perry, *Closer to the Light: Learning from the Near-Death Experiences of Children* (New York: Villard, 1990).

12. Morse with Perry, *Closer to the Light*, 116.

13. R. Moody and P. Perry, *The Light Beyond* (New York: Bantam Books, 1988), 10.

14. K. R. Rich, *The Red Devil: To Hell with Cancer—and Back* (New York: Crown, 1999), 22–23.

15. D. C. Johanson and B. Edgar, *From Lucy to Language* (New York: Simon and Schuster, 1996).

16. Some NDErs in particular have attributed male characteristics to these beings of light—in descriptions of either their facial appearance or their voice. A few have been described as female. Most have been described as having both gender characteristics, or none.

17. S. P. Muthumana, M. Kumari, A. Kellehear, S. Kumar, and F. Moosa, "Deathbed Visions from India: A Study of Family Observations in Northern Kerala," *Omega: Journal of Death & Dying* 62, no. 2 (2010–2011): 104.

18. A. Kellehear, V. Pogonet, R. Mindruta-Stratan, and V. Gorelco, "Deathbed Visions from the Republic of Moldova: A Content Analysis of Family Observations," *Omega: Journal of Death & Dying* 64, no. 4 (2012): 303–317.

19. A. Kellehear, V. Pogonet, R. Mindruta-Stratan, and V. Gorelco, *Care of the Dying in the Republic of Moldova* (Chisinau: UNESCO, 2011), 85–86.

2. Hallucinations

1. An earlier version of this chapter appeared as A. Kellehear, "Unusual Perceptions at the End of Life: Limitations to the Diagnosis of Hallucina-

tions in Palliative Medicine," *BMJ Supportive and Palliative Care* 7, no. 3 (2017): 238–246.

2. B. Greyson and M. B. Leister, "Auditory Hallucinations Following Near-Death Experiences," *Journal of Humanistic Psychology* 44, no. 3 (2004): 320–336; J. M. Pierre, "Hallucinations in Nonpsychotic Disorders: Toward Differential Diagnosis of 'Hearing Voices,'" *Harvard Review of Psychiatry* 18, no. 1 (2010): 22–35.

3. D. Collerton, E. Perry, and I. McKeith, "Why People See Things That Are Not There: A Novel Perception and Attention Deficit Model for Recurrent Complex Visual Hallucination," *Behavioral and Brain Science* 28 (2005): 737–794.

4. P. Allen, F. Laroi, P. K. McGuire, and A. Aleman, "The Hallucinating Brain: A Review of Structural and Functional Neuroimaging Studies in Hallucinations," *Neuroscience and Behavioral Reviews* 32 (2008): 180.

5. D. K. Tracy and S. S. Shergill, "Mechanisms Underlying Auditory Hallucinations—Understanding Perception Without Stimulus," *Brain Sciences* 3 (2013): 642–669.

6. A. I. Langer, G. Stanghellini, A. J. Cangas, P. H. Lysaker, L. Nieto-Munoz, J. A. Moriana, M. L. Barrigon, and A. Ambrosini, "Interpretation, Emotional Reactions, and Daily Life Implications of Hallucination-Like Experiences in Clinical and Nonclinical Populations," *Psicothema* 27, no. 1 (2015): 19–25.

7. A. T. Beck and N. A. Rector, "A Cognitive Model of Hallucinations," *Cognitive Therapy and Research* 27, no. 1 (2003): 19–52.

8. J. van Os, R. J. Linscott, I. Myin-Germeys, P. Delespaul, and L. Krabbendam, "A Systematic Review and Meta-analysis of the Psychotic Continuum: Evidence for a Psychosis-Prone-Persistence-Impairment Model of Psychotic Disorder," *Psychological Medicine* 39 (2009): 179–195.

9. P. Allen, D. Freeman, P. McGuire, P. Garety, E. Kuipers, D. Fowler, P. Bebbington, C. Green, G. Dunn, and K. Ray, "The Prediction of Hallucinatory Predisposition in Non-clinical Individuals: Examining the Contribution of Emotion and Reasoning," *British Journal of Clinical Psychology* 44 (2005): 127–132; F. Laroi, T. M. Luhmann, V. Bell, W. A. Christian, S. Deshpande, C. Fernyhough, J. Jenkins, and A. Woods, "Culture and Hallucinations: Overview and Future Directions," *Schizophrenia Bulletin* 40, no. 4 (2014): S213–S220.

10. V. Beavan, J. Read, and C. Cartwright, "The Prevalence of Voice-Hearers in the General Population: A Literature Review," *Journal of Mental Health* 20, no. 3 (2011): 281–292.

11. H. Temmingh, D. J. Stein, S. Seedat, and D. R. Williams, "The Prevalence and Correlates of Hallucinations in a General Population Sample: Findings from the South African Stress and Health Study," *African Journal of Psychiatry* 14 (2011): 211–217.

12. R. J. Linscott and J. van Os, "An Updated and Conservative Systematic Review and Meta-analysis of Epidemiological Evidence on Psychotic Experiences in Children and Adults: On the Pathway from Proneness to Persistence to Dimensional Expression Across Mental Disorders," *Psychological Medicine* 43 (2013): 1133–1149.

13. F. Laroi, P. Marczewski, and M. Van der Linden, "Further Evidence of the Multidimensionality of Hallucinatory Predisposition: Factor Structure of a Modified Version of the Launay-Slade Hallucinations Scale in a Normal Population," *European Psychiatry* 19 (2004): 15–20.

14. G. Gibson, P. G. Mottram, D. J. Burn, J. V. Hindle, S. Landua, M. Samuel, C. S. Hurt, R. G. Brown, and K. C. M. Wilson, "Frequency, Prevalence, Incidence, and Risk Factors Associated with Visual Hallucinations in a Sample of Patients with Parkinson's Disease: A Longitudinal 4-Year Study," *Geriatric Psychiatry* 28 (2013): 626–631.

15. N. J. Diederich, C. G. Goetz, and G. T. Stebbins, "Repeated Visual Hallucinations in Parkinson's Disease as Disturbed External/Internal Perceptions: Focused Review and a New Integrated Model," *Movement Disorders* 20, no. 2 (2005): 130–140.

16. S. Chaudhury, "Hallucinations: Clinical Aspects and Management," *Industrial Psychiatry Journal* 19, no. 1 (2010): 5–12.

17. R. S. Wilson, Y. Tang, N. T. Aggarwal, D. W. Gilley, J. J. McCann, J. L. Bienias, and D. A. Evans, "Hallucinations, Cognitive Decline, and Death in Alzheimer's Disease," *Neuroepidemiology* 26 (2006): 68–75.

18. C. L. Regnard and S. Tempest, *Managing Opioid Adverse Effects: A Guide to Symptom Relief in Advanced Disease*, 4th ed. (Hale, UK: Hochland and Hochland, 1998).

19. A. Fountain, "Visual Hallucinations: A Prevalence Study Among Hospice Inpatients," *Palliative Medicine* 15 (2001): 19–25.

20. J. Walker, C. Holm Hanson, P. Martin, A. Sawhney, P. Thekkumpurath, C. Beale, S. Symeonides, L. Wall, G. Murray, and M. Sharpe, "Prevalence of Depression in Adults with Cancer: A Systematic Review," *Annals of Oncology* 24, no. 4 (2012): 895–900.

21. M. M. Ohayon and A. F. Schatzberg, "Prevalence of Depressive Episodes with Psychotic Features in the General Population," *American Journal of Psychiatry* 159, no. 11 (2002): 1855–1861.

22. W. S. Breitbart and Y. Alici, *Psychosocial Palliative Care* (New York: Oxford University Press, 2014).

23. Fountain, "Visual Hallucinations."

24. J. Holden, B. Greyson, and D. James, *The Handbook of Near-Death Experiences: 30 Years of Investigation* (Santa Barbara, CA: Praeger, 2009).

2. Hallucinations

25. P. van Lommel, "About the Continuity of Consciousness," *Advances in Experimental Medicine and Biology* 550 (2004): 115–132.

26. S. Brayne, C. Farnham, and P. Fenwick, "Deathbed Phenomena and Their Effect on a Palliative Care Team: A Pilot Study," *American Journal of Hospice and Palliative Care* 23, no. 1 (2006): 17–24; P. Fenwick, H. Lovelace, and S. Brayne, "Comfort for the Dying: Five Year Retrospective and One Year Prospective Studies of End of Life Experiences," *Archives of Gerontology and Geriatrics* 51, no. 2 (2010): 173–179; P. Fenwick and S. Brayne, "End of Life Experiences: Reaching Out for Compassion, Communication and Connection-Meaning of Deathbed Visions and Coincidences," *American Journal of Hospice and Palliative Care* 28, no. 1 (2011): 7–15.

27. Fountain, "Visual Hallucinations."

28. S. P. Muthumana, M. Kumari, A. Kellehear, S. Kumar, and F. Moosa, "Deathbed Visions from India: A Study of Family Observations in Northern Kerala," *Omega: Journal of Death & Dying* 62, no. 2 (2010–2011): 95–107.

29. A. Kellehear, V. Pogonet, R. Mindruta-Stratan, and V. Gorelco, "Deathbed Visions from the Republic of Moldova: A Content Analysis of Family Observations," *Omega: Journal of Death & Dying* 64, no. 4 (2012): 303–317.

30. A. Fountain and A. Kellehear, "On Prevalence Disparities in Recent Empirical Studies of Deathbed Visions," *Journal of Palliative Care* 28, no. 2 (2012): 113–115.

31. Pierre, "Hallucinations in Nonpsychotic Disorders."

32. Tracy and Shergill, "Mechanisms Underlying Auditory Hallucinations."

33. Pierre, "Hallucinations in Nonpsychotic Disorders."

34. M. E. Carlsson and I. M. Nilsson, "Bereaved Spouses' Adjustment After the Patients' Death in Palliative Care," *Palliative and Supportive Care* 5 (2007): 397–404.

35. Beavan, Read, and Cartwright, "Prevalence of Voice-Hearers in the General Population."

36. Laroi et al., "Culture and Hallucinations."

37. In this book I refer to reports by the bereaved concerning contact with their dead as "visions of the bereaved." Other writers refer to these experiences as "hallucinations of the bereaved" or "after-death communication." The term *vision* is a common descriptor in the religious and folk studies literature and allows us to link these kinds of experiences to other, possibly related, phenomena such as crisis apparitions, Marian visionary experiences, and so on. More importantly, for me anyway, it maintains the emphasis on the one who perceives and makes no judgment concerning origins. The term *hallucination* seems to fly the flag for those who would too readily pathologize these perceptions, while the phrase *after-death communication* is too

readily linked to those invested in paranormal explanations. Furthermore, the term *after-death communication* also deflects attention away from the importance of the relationship between the dead and the one who perceives, and in this way potentially conflates encounters between parties known to each other with other unrelated encounters with unknown parties (hauntings, ghost stories, Ouija encounters, and so on). In specifically referring to the circumstance of bereavement, I am drawing attention to the importance of a prior relationship as the main basis for the contact.

38. Greyson and Leister, "Auditory Hallucinations Following Near-Death Experiences"; L. S. Betty, "Are They Hallucinations or Are They Real? The Spirituality of Deathbed and Near-Death Visions," *Omega: Journal of Death & Dying* 53, nos. 1–2 (2006): 37–49; Kellehear et al., "Deathbed Visions from the Republic of Moldova."

39. R. K. Siegal, "The Psychology of Life After Death," *American Psychologist* 35, no. 10 (1980): 911–931; A. M. Ethier, "Death-Related Sensory Experiences," *Journal of Pediatric Oncology Nursing* 22, no. 2 (2005): 104–111; F. Varese, E. Barkus, and R. P. Bentall, "Dissociation Mediates the Relationship Between Childhood Trauma and Hallucination-Proneness," *Psychological Medicine* 42 (2005): 1025–1036.

40. E. Kasten and J. S. Geier, "Near-Death Experiences: Between Spiritual Transmigration and Psychopathological Hallucinations," *Journal of Studies in Social Sciences* 9, no. 1 (2014): 34–82.

41. B. S. Kasper, E. M. Kasper, E. Pauli, and H. Stefan, "Phenomenology of Hallucinations, Illusions and Delusions as Part of Seizure Semiology," *Epilepsy and Behavior* 18 (2010): 13–23.

42. S. Blackmore, *Dying to Live: Science and the Near-Death Experience* (London: Grafton, 1993); D. Mobbs and C. Watt, "There Is Nothing Paranormal About Near-Death Experiences: How Neuroscience Can Explain Seeing Bright Lights, Meeting the Dead, or Being Convinced You Are One of Them," *Trends in Cognitive Sciences* 15, no. 10 (1993): 447–449.

43. J. Borg, *Cacti* (London: Blandford Press, 1970).

44. Pierre, "Hallucinations in Nonpsychotic Disorders"; J. D. Blom, *A Dictionary of Hallucinations* (Dordrecht: Springer, 2010); A. Woods, N. Jones, M. Bernini, F. Callard, B. Alderson-Day, J. C. Badcock, V. Bell, C. C. H. Cook, T. Csordas, C. Humpston, et al., "Interdisciplinary Approaches to the Phenomenology of Auditory Verbal Hallucinations," *Schizophrenia Bulletin* 40, no. 4 (2014): S246–S254.

45. C. McCreery, "Perception and Hallucination: The Case for Continuity" (Oxford Forum, Philosophical Paper No. 2006-1, 2006); C. Pelling, "Characterizing Hallucinations Epistemically," *Synthese* 178 (2011): 437–459.

46. McCreery, "Perception and Hallucination."

47. K. Hill and D. E. J. Linden, "Hallucinatory Experiences in Non-clinical Populations," in *The Neuroscience of Hallucinations*, ed. R. Jardini, A. Cachia, P. Thomas, and D. Pins (New York: Springer, 2013), 21–41; Woods et al., "Interdisciplinary Approaches to the Phenomenology of Auditory Verbal Hallucinations."

48. J. Watkins, *Hearing Voices: A Common Human Experience* (Melbourne: Hill of Content, 1998); Greyson and Leister, "Auditory Hallucinations Following Near-Death Experiences"; S. McCarthy-Jones, T. Trauer, A. MacKinnon, E. Sims, N. Thomas, and D. L. Copolov, "A New Phenomenological Survey of Auditory Hallucinations: Evidence for Subtypes and Implications for Theory and Practice," *Schizophrenia Bulletin* 40, no. 1 (2014): 225–235.

49. S. Kumar, S. Soren, and S. Chaudhury, "Hallucinations: Etiology and Clinical Implications," *Industrial Psychiatry Journal* 18, no. 2 (2009): 119–126.

50. Pierre, "Hallucinations in Nonpsychotic Disorders."

51. Laroi et al., "Culture and Hallucinations."

52. D. Freeman and P. A. Garety, "Connecting Neurosis and Psychosis: The Direct Influence of Emotion on Delusions and Hallucinations," *Behavioral Research and Therapy* 41 (2003): 923–947.

53. Beavan, Read, and Cartwright, "Prevalence of Voice-Hearers in the General Population."

54. A. P. Morrison, "The Interpretations of Intrusions in Psychosis: An Integrative Cognitive Approach to Hallucinations and Delusions," *Behavioral and Cognitive Psychotherapy* 29 (2001): 257–276; L. C. Johns, "Hallucinations in the General Population," *Current Psychiatric Reports* 7 (2005): 162–167; Tracy and Shergill, "Mechanisms Underlying Auditory Hallucinations"; Laroi et al., "Culture and Hallucinations."

55. P. Delespaul, M. deVries, and J. van Os, "Determinants of Occurrence and Recovery from Hallucinations in Daily Life," *Psychiatry and Psychiatric Epidemiology* 37 (2002): 97–104.

56. Chaudhury, "Hallucinations."

57. C. Steel, G. Haddock, N. Tarrier, A. Picken, and C. Barrowclough, "Auditory Hallucinations and Post-traumatic Stress Disorder with Schizophrenia and Substance Abuse Disorder," *Journal of Nervous and Mental Disease* 199, no. 9 (2011): 709–711.

58. S. Cottam, S. N. Paul, O. J. Doughty, L. Carpenter, A. Al-Mousawi, S. Karvounis, and D. J. Done, "Does Religious Belief Enable Positive Interpretation of Auditory Hallucinations? A Comparison of Religious Voice-Hearers With and Without Psychosis," *Cognitive Neuropsychiatry* 16, no. 5 (2011):

403–421; R. E. Gearing, D. Alonso, A. Smolak, K. McHugh, S. Harmon, and S. Baldwin, "Association of Religion with Delusions and Hallucinations in the Context of Schizophrenia: Implications for Engagement and Adherence," *Schizophrenia Research* 126 (2011): 150–163.

59. Tracy and Shergill, "Mechanisms Underlying Auditory Hallucinations."

60. B. Elliott, E. Joyce, and S. Shorvon, "Delusions, Illusions and Hallucinations in Epilepsy: Elementary Phenomena," *Epilepsy Research* 85 (2009): 162–171.

61. Hill and Linden, "Hallucinatory Experiences in Non-clinical Populations."

62. Allen, Laroi, et al., "The Hallucinating Brain."

63. Hill and Linden, "Hallucinatory Experiences in Non-clinical Populations."

64. Elliott, Joyce, and Shorvon, "Delusions, Illusions and Hallucinations in Epilepsy."

65. Collerton, Perry, and McKeith, "Why People See Things That Are Not There."

66. Tracy and Shergill, "Mechanisms Underlying Auditory Hallucinations."

67. Mobbs and Watt, "There Is Nothing Paranormal About Near-Death Experiences," 448.

68. J. M. Windt, "Altered Consciousness in Philosophy," in *Altering Consciousness: Multidisciplinary Perspectives*, ed. E. Cardena and M. Winkelman (Santa Barbara, CA: Praeger, 2011), 229–254.

69. A. Kellehear, *Experiences Near Death: Beyond Medicine and Religion* (New York: Oxford University Press, 1996).

70. J. Borjigin, U. Lee, T. Liu, D. Pal, S. Huff, D. Klarr, J. Sloboda, J. Hernandez, M. M. Wang, and G. A. Mashour, "Surge of Neurophysiological Coherence and Connectivity in the Dying Brain," *Proceedings of the National Academy of Sciences* 110, no. 35 (2013): 14432–14437; D. Li, O. S. Mabrouk, T. Lui, F. Tian, G. Xu, S. Rengifo, S. J. Choi, A. Mathur, C. P. Crooks, R. T. Kennedy, et al., "Asphyxia-Activated Cortico-Cardiac Signaling Accelerates Onset of Cardiac Arrest," *Proceedings of the National Academy of Science* 112, no. 16 (2015): E2073–E2082.

71. C. Zaleski, *Otherworld Journeys: Accounts of Near-Death Experience in Medieval and Modern Times* (New York: Oxford University Press, 1987); A. Kellehear, "The Near-Death Experience as Status Passage," *Social Science & Medicine* 31, no. 8 (1990): 933–939.

72. Fountain, "Visual Hallucinations."

73. Kasten and Geier, "Near-Death Experiences."

74. E. Leslie, *Desperate Journeys, Abandoned Souls: True Stories of Castaways and Other Survivors* (London: Macmillan, 1988); D. Barnard, A. Towers,

P. Boston, and Y. Lambrinidou, *Crossing Over: Narratives of Palliative Care* (New York: Oxford University Press, 2000); A. Kellehear, *The Inner Life of the Dying Person* (New York: Columbia University Press, 2014).

75. Kumar, Soren, and Chaudhury, "Hallucinations."

76. Woods et al., "Interdisciplinary Approaches to the Phenomenology of Auditory Verbal Hallucinations."

77. L. Blackman, *Hearing Voices: Embodiment and Experience* (London: Free Association Books, 2001); McCarthy-Jones et al., "A New Phenomenological Survey of Auditory Hallucinations"; O. Sacks, *Hallucinations* (London: Picador, 2013).

78. Hill and Linden, "Hallucinatory Experiences in Non-clinical Populations"; E. Faccio, D. Romaioli, J. Dagani, and S. Cipolletta, "Auditory Hallucinations as a Personal Experience: Analysis of Non-psychiatric Voice Hearers' Narration," *Journal of Psychiatric and Mental Health Nursing* 20 (2013): 761–767.

79. Beavan, Read, and Cartwright, "Prevalence of Voice-Hearers in the General Population."

80. I. Al-Issa, "The Illusion of Reality or the Reality of Illusion: Hallucinations and Culture," *British Journal of Psychiatry* 166 (1995): 368.

81. Pierre, "Hallucinations in Nonpsychotic Disorders."

82. Pierre, "Hallucinations in Nonpsychotic Disorders," 33.

83. Windt, "Altered Consciousness in Philosophy."

84. W. James, *The Varieties of Religious Experience* (London: Fontana, 1960).

85. G. Shushan, *Conceptions of the Afterlife in Early Civilizations* (London: Continuum, 2009); M. Fox, *Religion, Spirituality, and the Near-Death Experience* (London: Routledge, 2003).

86. Windt, "Altered Consciousness in Philosophy."

3. Perception

1. List25 Team, "25 Insane Optical Illusions That Will Leave You Dazed and Confused," List25, https://list25.com/25-incredible-optical-illusions/, accessed January 2, 2020.

2. J. Friedenberg, *Visual Attention and Consciousness* (New York: Psychology Press, 2013), 8.

3. R. R. Hunt and H. C. Ellis, *Fundamentals of Cognitive Psychology*, 7th ed. (New York: McGraw-Hill, 2004).

4. Hunt and Ellis, *Fundamentals of Cognitive Psychology*, 39.

5. Hunt and Ellis, *Fundamentals of Cognitive Psychology*, 73–74.

3. Perception

6. E. B. Goldstein, *Cognitive Psychology* (Belmont, CA: Thomson Wadsworth, 2008), 57–58.

7. Goldstein, *Cognitive Psychology*, 231.

8. R. Blake and R. Sekular, *Perception* (New York: McGraw-Hill, 2006); M. Kastanakis and B. G. Voyer, "The Effect of Culture on Perception and Cognition: A Conceptual Framework," *Journal of Business Research* 67, no. 4 (2014): 425–433.

9. R. T. Carroll, *The Skeptic's Dictionary*, 1994, http://skepdic.com/apophenia.html.

10. T. G. West, *Seeing What Others Cannot See: The Hidden Advantages of Visual Thinkers and Differently Wired Brains* (New York: Prometheus Books, 2017).

11. C. C. Carbon, "Understanding Human Perception by Human-Made Illusion," *Frontiers in Human Neuroscience* 8, no. 566 (2014): 5, doi: 10.3389/fnhum.2014.00566.

12. A. Kellehear, *The Inner Life of the Dying Person* (New York: Columbia University Press, 2014).

13. K. Wright, "Relationships with Death: The Terminally Ill Talk About Dying," *Journal of Marital and Family Therapy* 29, no. 4 (2003): 450–451.

14. V. Frankl, *Man's Search for Meaning* (London: Hodder & Stoughton, 1964), 90.

15. S. Freud, *Reflections on War and Death* (New York: Moffat, Yard & Co., 1918), 67.

16. S. P. Muthumana, M. Kumari, A. Kellehear, S. Kumar, and F. Moosa, "Deathbed Visions from India: A Study of Family Observations in Northern Kerala," *Omega: Journal of Death & Dying* 62, no. 2 (2010–2011): 105.

17. P. van Lommel, "About the Continuity of Consciousness," *Advances in Experimental Medicine and Biology* 550 (2004): 115–132.

4. Greetings and Other Customs

1. This story is used with permission and has been anonymized. Sally is not her real name.

2. In this book I confine myself to contact with mainly the adult dead including the older child. I am aware that deceased adults are obviously not the only dead who contact us. Past animal companions and younger children such as stillborn infants and those who died shortly after birth have also reportedly made contact. However, the methods of contact by these groups are often different and sometimes mediated by others.

3. R. Firth, "Verbal and Bodily Greetings and Partings," in *The Interpretation of Ritual: Essays in Honour of A. I. Richards*, ed. J. S. La Fontaine (London: Routledge, 1972), 30–31.

4. E. Goody, "'Greeting,' 'Begging,' and the Presentation of Respect," in *The Interpretation of Ritual: Essays in Honour of A. I. Richards*, ed. J. S. La Fontaine (London: Routledge, 1972), 39–71.

5. G. Aston, "What's a Public Service Encounter Anyway?," in *Negotiating Service: Studies in the Discourse of Bookshop Encounters*, ed. G. Aston (Bologna, Italy: Cooperativa Libraria Universitaria Editrice, 1988), 25–42.

6. C. Beal and V. Traverso, "'Hello, We're Outrageously Punctual': Front Door Rituals Between Friends in Australia and France," *French Language Studies* 20 (2010): 17–29.

7. B. Guggenheim and J. Guggenheim, *Hello from Heaven* (New York: Bantam, 1996).

8. Guggenheim and Guggenheim, *Hello from Heaven*, 92.

9. K. Ring, *Life at Death: A Scientific Investigation of the Near-Death Experience* (New York: Coward, McCann & Geoghegan, 1980), 63–64.

10. M. Morse with P. Perry, *Closer to the Light: Learning from the Near-Death Experiences of Children* (New York, Villard, 1990); R. Moody and P. Perry, *The Light Beyond* (New York: Bantam Books, 1988).

11. Moody and Perry, *The Light Beyond*, 10.

12. Morse with Perry, *Closer to the Light*, 112.

13. K. R. Rich, *The Red Devil: To Hell with Cancer—and Back* (New York: Crown, 1999), 22–23.

14. A. Kellehear, *Dying of Cancer: The Final Year of Life* (Churs, Switzerland: Harwood Academic Publishers, 1990).

15. G. Simmel, "Note on Faithfulness and Gratitude," in *The Sociology of George Simmel*, ed. K. H. Wolff (New York: Free Press, 1950), 379–395.

16. B. Malinowski, *Magic, Science and Religion* (New York: Free Press, 1948).

17. M. L. Knapp, R. P. Hart, G. W. Friedrich, and G. M. Shulman, "The Rhetoric of Good-Bye: Verbal and Non-verbal Correlates of Leave Taking," *Speech Monographs* 40 (1973): 182–198.

5. Advice

1. In the Catholic Bible, Acts 22; in the Protestant version, Acts 9.

2. In most accounts, this being of light identifies itself as Jesus. This is unusual self-identification for a being of light, since there are so many of them

5. Advice

(certainly in modern near-death accounts). And we have accounts where several beings of light stand side by side. Most of these beings do not identify themselves by name—this is a fact so far as we can glean this from the pattern of recent accounts. This means that they cannot all be Jesus, unless there is some sort of hall-of-mirrors effect, or that one of them really is/was Jesus and that particular one zoomed in on Saul. Both fantastic options are theoretically possible. We just do not, and probably cannot, know this kind of detail drawing merely on this single story.

3. Saeed Kamali Dehghan, "Iranian Killer's Execution Halted at Last Minute by Victim's Parents," *The Guardian*, April 16, 2014, http://www.theguardian.com/world/2014/apr/16/iran-parents-halt-killer-execution.

4. Dehghan, "Iranian Killer's Execution Halted at Last Minute by Victim's Parents."

5. O. Felek and A. Knysh, eds., *Dreams and Visions in Islamic Societies* (Albany: State University of New York Press, 2012).

6. J. Frazer, *The Belief in Immortality and the Worship of the Dead*, 3 vols. (London: Macmillan, 1911–1924).

7. R. C. Finucane, *Ghosts* (New York: Prometheus Books, 1996), 75.

8. Finucane, *Ghosts*, 223.

9. Frazer, *The Belief in Immortality*, 2:241.

10. "Ever Sense the Presence of a Deceased Loved One?," City-Data.com, http://www.city-data.com/forum/unexplained-mysteries-paranormal/1564889-ever-sense-presence-deceased-loved-one-4.html, accessed January 2, 2020.

11. *Pareschatology* as a term refers to the *first* things that happen to a soul or spirit immediately after death. This is different from the term *eschatology*, which refers to the *last* things the soul or spirit will encounter on its postdeath journey—heaven, hell, reincarnation, and so on.

12. E. Alexander, *Proof of Heaven: A Neurosurgeon's Journey into the Afterlife* (New York: Simon and Schuster, 2012).

13. B. Malinowski, *Magic, Science and Religion* (New York: Free Press, 1948), 161.

14. D. A. Counts, "Near-Death and Out of Body Experiences in a Melanesian Society," *Anabiosis* 3 (1983): 115–135. See also J. T. Green, "Near-Death Experiences in Chommorro Culture," *Vital Signs* 4 (1984): 1–2, 6–7.

15. R. Moody, *Life After Life* (New York: Bantam, 1970).

16. K. Ring, *Life at Death: A Scientific Investigation of the Near-Death Experience* (New York: Coward, McCann & Geoghegan, 1980).

17. C. Zaleski, *Otherworld Journeys: Accounts of Near-Death Experience in Medieval and Modern Times* (New York: Oxford University Press, 1987).

18. Ring, *Life at Death*, 84.

19. Zaleski, *Otherworld Journeys*, 132–133.
20. Ring, *Life at Death*, 85.
21. Finucane, *Ghosts*.
22. S. Freud, *The Future of an Illusion* (London: Hogarth Press, 1927); E. Durkheim, *The Elementary Forms of the Religious Life* (New York: Free Press, 1965); M. Weber, *The Sociology of Religion* (Boston: Beacon Press, 1965).
23. Malinowski, *Magic, Science and Religion*, 47–53.
24. Malinowski, *Magic, Science and Religion*, 47.
25. Malinowski, *Magic, Science and Religion*, 52.

6. Transformation

1. This story was originally published in one of my earlier books about death and loss, *Eternity and Me: The Everlasting Things in Life and Death* (Melbourne: Hill of Content, 2000).
2. K. Osis, *Deathbed Observations by Physicians and Nurses* (New York: Parapsychology Foundation, 1961); see also K. Osis and E. Haraldsson, *At the Hour of Our Death* (New York: Hastings House, 1977).
3. P. Fenwick, H. Lovelace, and S. Brayne, "End of Life Experiences and Their Implications for Palliative Care," *International Journal of Environment Studies* 64, no. 3 (2007): 320.
4. A. Kellehear, "The Near-Death Experience as Status Passage," *Social Science & Medicine* 31, no. 8 (1990): 933–939.
5. M. Grey, *Return from Death: An Exploration of the Near-Death Experience* (London: Arkana, 1985), 95.
6. K. Ring, *Life at Death: A Scientific Investigation of the Near-Death Experience* (New York: Coward, McCann & Geoghegan, 1980), 143.
7. C. Zaleski, *Otherworld Journeys: Accounts of Near-Death Experience in Medieval and Modern Times* (New York: Oxford University Press, 1987), 144.
8. Kellehear, "Near-Death Experience as Status Passage."
9. B. Guggenheim and J. Guggenheim, *Hello from Heaven* (New York: Bantam, 1996).
10. Guggenheim and Guggenheim, *Hello from Heaven*, 317.
11. Guggenheim and Guggenheim, *Hello from Heaven*, 319.
12. Guggenheim and Guggenheim, *Hello from Heaven*, 319.
13. A. van Gennep, *The Rites of Passage* (1908; repr., London: Routledge & Kegan Paul, 1960).
14. S. T. Kimball, introduction to *The Rites of Passage*, by A. van Gennep (London: Routledge & Kegan Paul, 1960), vii.

15. Kimball, introduction to *The Rites of Passage*, xvii.

16. K. R, Rich, *The Red Devil: To Hell with Cancer—and Back* (New York: Crown, 1999), 22–23.

17. "[Serious] Redditors Who Have Been Clinically Dead and Then Revived/Resuscitated: What Did Dying Feel Like? Did You See Anything Whilst Passed On?," Reddit, https://www.reddit.com/r/AskReddit/comments/332k1c/serious_redditors_who_have_been_clinically_dead/cqh8t7e, accessed January 2, 2020.

18. "[Serious] Redditors Who Have Been Clinically Dead."

19. H. D. Thoreau, *Walden* (1854; repr., New York: Houghton Mifflin, 1906), 8.

20. "[Serious] Redditors Who Have Been Clinically Dead."

7. Gifts

1. E. Kübler-Ross, *On Death and Dying* (New York: Macmillan, 1969).

2. I cannot help but be reminded of similar religious experiences that I had read about before this incident. For example, the psychologist James Leuba recounts the case of a man who was feeling well and walking in the French Alps quite happily with his friends when "he is suddenly overtaken by a throb of emotion so violent, so powerful, that he had to sit down and motion to his companions to continue without him for a while. The emotions were overwhelmingly positive, so joyous that he began to weep uncontrollably for a few minutes. He was convinced he was in the presence of the Christian god. 'God was present, though invisible; He fell under no one of my senses, yet my consciousness perceived Him.'" According to Leuba, this is a classical St. Paul moment—going about one's usual business, feeling oneself in no unusual way physically or emotionally but being 'struck down' as it were by high uncontrollable positive emotion and being suddenly aware—if aware is the right word—of a sense of a divine presence. This is a paraphrase of the case from J. H. Leuba, *The Psychology of Religious Mysticism* (London: Routledge, 1925), 210. The experiential similarity of this case with my own is striking to me. Obviously my own experience was less intense and disabling, and I did not sense that a god was animating me, but rather an old and recently dead friend. Notwithstanding these differences, my experience is clearly part of this broader pattern of unprecedented spontaneous, powerful (i.e., power-filled), and inexplicably joyous communication.

3. Interestingly, the observation I make here is that not only did I not "see" Heather, but I also did not "hear" her either. This personal experience for me is a critical check against dividing up mystical encounters simplistically between

7. Gifts

seeing and hearing—sometimes we might get "messages" as a kind of intrusive "thought insertion." These might be similar to communications in some types of dreams. See J. Miller, *Convinced That God Has Called Us: Dreams, Visions and the Perception of God's Will in Luke-Acts* (Leiden: Brill, 2007).

4. C. Dickens, *A Christmas Carol* (London: Chapman & Hall, 1843).

5. J. Posner, "Death as a Courtesy Stigma," *Essence* 1, no. 1 (1976): 39–50.

6. BBC News, "James Corden Tears Up at Paul McCartney's Carpool Karaoke," June 22, 2018, https://www.bbc.co.uk/news/entertainment-arts-44576629.

7. BBC News, "My Best Friend's Killer Got Away—Until I Made Police Try Again," June 26, 2018, https://www.bbc.co.uk/news/stories-44470377.

8. S. P. Muthumana, M. Kumari, A. Kellehear, S. Kumar, and F. Moosa, "Deathbed Visions from India: A Study of Family Observations in Northern Kerala," *Omega: Journal of Death & Dying* 62, no. 2 (2010–2011): 97–109.

9. A. Kellehear, V. Pogonet, R. Mindruta-Stratan, and V. Gorelco, "Deathbed Visions from the Republic of Moldova: A Content Analysis of Family Observations," *Omega: Journal of Death & Dying* 64, no. 4 (2011–2012): 303–317.

10. Kellehear et al., "Deathbed Visions from the Republic of Moldova," 310.

11. Kellehear et al., "Deathbed Visions from the Republic of Moldova," 310–311.

12. Kellehear et al., "Deathbed Visions from the Republic of Moldova," 311.

13. Kellehear et al., "Deathbed Visions from the Republic of Moldova," 312.

14. Kellehear et al., "Deathbed Visions from the Republic of Moldova," 313.

15. K. Ring, "Amazing Grace: The Near-Death Experience as Compensatory Gift," *Journal of Near-Death Studies* 10, no. 1 (1991): 11–39.

16. M. Callanan and P. Kelly, *Final Gifts: Understanding the Special Awareness, Needs, and Communications of the Dying* (New York: Bantam, 2012).

17. S. F. Linn, D. Linn, and M. Linn, *The Gifts of the Near-Death Experience* (Newburyport, MA: Hampton Roads, 2016).

18. International Association for Near Death Studies, "It Marked the Trajectory of My Life," January 5, 2017, https://iands.org/research/nde-research/nde-archives31/newest-accounts/1184-it-marked-the-trajectory-of-my-life.html.

19. International Association for Near Death Studies, "I Am a Bird, and Thus Starts My Life," November 16, 2016, https://iands.org/research/nde-research/nde-archives31/newest-accounts/1177-i-am-a-bird-and-thus-starts-my-life.html.

20. R. W. Putsch, "Ghost Illness: A Cross-Cultural Experience with the Expression of a Non-Western Tradition in Clinical Practice," *American Indian and Alaska Mental Health Research* 2, no. 2 (1988): 6–26.

21. *Oxford English Dictionary*, s.v. "Gift *(n.)*," https://en.oxforddictionaries.com/definition/gift, accessed January 2, 2020.

22. *Online Etymology Dictionary*, s.v. "Gift *(n.)*," https://www.etymonline.com/word/gift, accessed January 2, 2020.

23. M. Mauss, *The Gift: Forms and Functions in Archaic Societies* (Glencoe, IL: Free Press, 1954).

24. "Gift relation" means that the offering always implies an obligation—it automatically brings a specific type of "relation" into existence by its appearance.

25. Kellehear et al., "Deathbed Visions from the Republic of Moldova," 313.

8. Vigils

1. B. Morgan, *On Becoming God: Late Medieval Mysticism and the Modern Western Self* (New York: Fordham University Press, 2013).

2. A. de Saint-Exupéry, *The Little Prince* (New York: Reynal & Hitchcock, 1943), 64–65.

3. P. Bachelor, *Sorrow and Solace: The Social World of the Cemetery* (Amityville, NY: Baywood Publishing Company, 2004).

4. This argument first appeared in my article "Vigils for the Dying: Origin and Functions of a Persistent Tradition," *Illness, Crisis & Loss* 21, no. 2 (2013): 109–124.

5. M. I. Berman, "The Todeserwartung Syndrome," *Geriatrics* 21 (1966): 187–192. See also S. Page and C. Komaromy, "Professional Performance: The Case of Unexpected and Expected Deaths," *Mortality* 10, no. 4 (2005): 294–307.

6. J. E. Seymour, "Revisiting Medicalization and 'Natural' Death," *Social Science & Medicine* 49, no. 5 (1999): 691–704. See also I. Fridh, A. Forsberg, and I. Bergbom, "Close Relatives' Experiences of Caring and of Physical Environment When a Loved One Dies in an ICU," *Intensive and Critical Care Nursing* 25 (2009): 111–119.

7. S. M. Donnelly and C. N. Donnelly, "The Experience of the Moment of Death in a Specialist Palliative Care Unit," *Irish Medical Journal* 102, no. 5 (2009): 143–149.

8. S. M. Donnelly, N. Michael, and C. Donnelly, "Experience of the Moment of Death at Home," *Mortality* 11, no. 4 (2005): 352–367.

9. For good examples of these support groups, see J. P. Carr and J. P. Fogarty, "Families at the Bedside: An Ethnographic Study of Vigilance," *Journal of Family Practice* 48, no. 6 (1999): 433–438; I. Fridh, I. Bergbom, and H. Haljamae, "No Going Back: Narratives by Close Relatives of the Brain Dead Patient,"

Intensive and Critical Care Nursing 17 (2001): 263–278; J. Woodhouse, "A Personal Reflection on Sitting at the Bedside of a Dying Loved One," *International Journal of Palliative Nursing* 10, no. 11 (2004): 537–541; Donnelly, Michael, and Donnelly, "Experience of the Moment of Death at Home"; A. Edmeads, "Watch with Me: A Chaplain's Perspective," *International Journal of Palliative Nursing* 13, no. 11 (2007): 549–553; T. Read and J. Wuest, "Daughters Caring for Dying Parents: A Process of Relinquishing," *Qualitative Health Research* 17, no. 7 (2007): 932–944.

10. Donnelly and Donnelly, "Experience of the Moment of Death in a Specialist Palliative Care Unit."

11. Fridh, Forsberg, Bergbom, "Close Relatives' Experiences of Caring," 115.

12. Donnelly and Donnelly, "Experience of the Moment of Death in a Specialist Palliative Care Unit," 144.

13. L. Freeman, M. Caserta, D. Lund, S. Rossa, A. Dowdy, and A. Partenheimer, "Music Thanatology: Prescriptive Harp Music as Palliative Care for the Dying Patient," *American Journal of Hospice and Palliative Care* 23, no. 2 (2006): 100–104.

14. Read and Wuest, "Daughters Caring for Dying Parents."

15. Woodhouse, "Personal Reflection on Sitting at the Bedside of a Dying Loved One."

16. Woodhouse, "Personal Reflection on Sitting at the Bedside of a Dying Loved One," 538.

17. Edmeads, "Watch with Me," 550.

18. See, for example, B. A. Chabner, "Cancer: A Personal Journey," *The Oncologist* 2, no. 4 (1997): 206–207; P. Wall, *Pain: The Science of Suffering* (London: Weidenfield & Nicholson, 1999); I. Craig, "Fear, Death and Sociology," *Mortality* 8, no. 3 (2003): 285–295.

19. L. Tolstoy, *The Death of Ivan Ilbyich* (1883; repr., New York: Bantam, 1981).

20. M. Albom, *Tuesdays with Morrie* (New York: Doubleday Books, 1997).

21. C. Wouters, "The Quest for New Rituals in Dying and Mourning: Changes in the We–I Balance," *Body and Society* 8, no. 1 (2002): 1–27.

22. R. K. Barnhart, *Chambers Dictionary of Etymology* (Edinburgh: H. W. Wilson, 1988), 1204, 1216.

23. V. Turner, *The Ritual Process: Structure and Anti-structure* (New York: Aldine de Gruyter, 1969), 95.

24. Turner, *The Ritual Process*, 106.

25. R. Grainger, *The Unburied* (Worthing, UK: Churchman Publishing, 1988), 55.

26. P. Lysaght, "Visible Death: Attitudes to the Dying in Ireland," *Marvels and Tales* 9, no. 1 (1995): 27–100; Woodhouse, "Personal Reflection on Sitting at the Bedside of a Dying Loved One."

27. See, for example, G. O. Crualaoich, "The Merry Wake," in *Irish Popular Culture 1650–1850*, ed. J. S. Donnelly and K. A. Miller (Dublin: Irish Academic Press, 1998), 173–200; P. Lysaght, "Hospitality at Wakes and Funerals in Ireland from the Seventeenth to the Nineteenth Century: Some Evidence from the Written Record," *Folklore* 114 (2003): 403–426; Woodhouse, "Personal Reflection on Sitting at the Bedside of a Dying Loved One."

28. Crualaoich, "The Merry Wake"; G. C. Gibson, *Wake Rites* (Gainesville: University Press of Florida, 2005).

29. Carr and Fogarty, "Families at the Bedside"; S. Donnelly and J. Battley, "Relative's Experience of the Moment of Death in a Tertiary Referral Hospital," *Mortality* 15, no. 1 (2010): 81–100.

Conclusion

1. F. Laroi, T. M. Luhmann, V. Bell, W. A. Christian, S. Deshpande, C. Fernyhough, J. Jenkins, and A. Woods, "Culture and Hallucinations: Overview and Future Directions," *Schizophrenia Bulletin* 40, no. 4 (2014): S214.

2. A personal communication that I first reported in A. Kellehear, *Eternity and Me: The Everlasting Things in Life and Death* (Melbourne: Hill of Content, 2000).

3. My view of my own efforts in this book mirror those of M. Mauss, *The Gift: Forms and Functions in Archaic Societies* (Glencoe, IL: Free Press, 1954), 76, when he spoke frankly about his own first work studying gift exchange: "We do not set this work up as a model; it simply proffers one or two suggestions. It is incomplete: the analysis could be pushed farther. We are really posing questions for historians and anthropologists and offering possible lines of research for them rather than resolving a problem and laying down definite answers. It is enough for us to be sure for the moment that we have given sufficient data for such an end."

Bibliography

Albom, M. *Tuesdays with Morrie*. New York: Doubleday, 1997.
Alexander, E. *Proof of Heaven: A Neurosurgeon's Journey into the Afterlife*. New York: Simon and Schuster, 2012.
Al-Issa, I. "The Illusion of Reality or the Reality of Illusion: Hallucinations and Culture." *British Journal of Psychiatry* 166 (1995): 368–373.
Allen, P., D. Freeman, P. McGuire, P. Garety, E. Kuipers, D. Fowler, P. Bebbington, C. Green, G. Dunn, and K. Ray. "The Prediction of Hallucinatory Predisposition in Non-clinical Individuals: Examining the Contribution of Emotion and Reasoning." *British Journal of Clinical Psychology* 44 (2005): 127–132.
Allen, P., F. Laroi, P. K. McGuire, and A. Aleman. "The Hallucinating Brain: A Review of Structural and Functional Neuroimaging Studies in Hallucinations." *Neuroscience and Behavioral Reviews* 32 (2008): 175–191.
Aston, G. "What's a Public Service Encounter Anyway?" In *Negotiating Service: Studies in the Discourse of Bookshop Encounters*, ed. G. Aston, 25–42. Bologna, Italy: Cooperativa Libraria Universitaria Editrice, 1988.
Bachelor, P. *Sorrow and Solace: The Social World of the Cemetery*. Amityville, NY: Baywood Publishing Company, 2004.
Barnard, D., A. Towers, P. Boston, and Y. Lambrinidou. *Crossing Over: Narratives of Palliative Care*. New York: Oxford University Press, 2000.
Barnhart, R. K. *Chambers Dictionary of Etymology*. Edinburgh: H. W. Wilson, 1988.

Bibliography

Barrett, W. *Deathbed Visions.* 1926. Repr., Wellingborough, UK: Aquarian Press, 1989.

BBC News. "James Corden Tears Up at Paul McCartney's Carpool Karaoke." June 22, 2018. https://www.bbc.co.uk/news/entertainment-arts-44576629.

———. "My Best Friend's Killer Got Away—Until I Made Police Try Again." June 26, 2018. https://www.bbc.co.uk/news/stories-44470377.

Beal, C., and V. Traverso. "'Hello, We're Outrageously Punctual': Front Door Rituals Between Friends in Australia and France." *French Language Studies* 20 (2010): 17–29.

Beavan, V., J. Read, and C. Cartwright. "The Prevalence of Voice-Hearers in the General Population: A Literature Review." *Journal of Mental Health* 20, no. 3 (2011): 281–292.

Beck, A. T., and N. A. Rector. "A Cognitive Model of Hallucinations." *Cognitive Therapy and Research* 27, no. 1 (2003): 19–52.

Berman, M. I. "The Todeserwartung Syndrome." *Geriatrics* 21 (1966): 187–192.

Betty, L. S. "Are They Hallucinations or Are They Real? The Spirituality of Deathbed and Near-Death Visions." *Omega: Journal of Death & Dying* 53, nos. 1–2 (2006): 37–49.

Blackman, L. *Hearing Voices: Embodiment and Experience.* London: Free Association Books, 2001.

Blackmore, S. *Dying to Live: Science and the Near-Death Experience.* London: Grafton, 1993.

Blake, R., and R. Sekular. *Perception.* New York: McGraw-Hill, 2006.

Blanes, R., and D. E. Santo, eds. *The Social Life of Spirits.* Chicago: University of Chicago Press, 2014.

Blom, J. D. *A Dictionary of Hallucinations.* Dordrecht: Springer, 2010.

Borg, J. *Cacti.* London: Blandford Press, 1970.

Borjigin, J., U. Lee, T. Liu, D. Pal, S. Huff, D. Klarr, J. Sloboda, J. Hernandez, M. M. Wang, and G. A. Mashour. "Surge of Neurophysiological Coherence and Connectivity in the Dying Brain." *Proceedings of the National Academy of Sciences* 110, no. 35 (2013): 14432–14437.

Brayne, S., C. Farnham, and P. Fenwick. "Deathbed Phenomena and Their Effect on a Palliative Care Team: A Pilot Study." *American Journal of Hospice and Palliative Care* 23, no. 1 (2006): 17–24.

Breitbart, W. S., and Y. Alici. *Psychosocial Palliative Care.* New York: Oxford University Press, 2014.

Callanan, M., and P. Kelly. *Final Gifts: Understanding the Special Awareness, Needs, and Communications of the Dying.* New York: Bantam, 2012.

Carbon, C. C. "Understanding Human Perception by Human-Made Illusion." *Frontiers in Human Neuroscience* 8, no. 566 (2014): 1–6. doi: 10.3389/fnhum.2014.00566.

Carlsson, M. E., and I. M. Nilsson. "Bereaved Spouses' Adjustment After the Patients' Death in Palliative Care." *Palliative and Supportive Care* 5 (2007): 397–404.

Carr, J. P., and J. P. Fogarty. "Families at the Bedside: An Ethnographic Study of Vigilance." *Journal of Family Practice* 48, no. 6 (1999): 433–438.

Carroll, R. T. *The Skeptic's Dictionary.* 1994. http://skepdic.com/apophenia.html.

Chabner, B. A. "Cancer: A Personal Journey." *The Oncologist* 2, no. 4 (1997): 206–207.

Chaudhury, S. "Hallucinations: Clinical Aspects and Management." *Industrial Psychiatry Journal* 19, no. 1 (2010): 5–12.

City-Data.com. "Ever Sense the Presence of a Deceased Loved One?" http://www.city-data.com/forum/unexplained-mysteries-paranormal/1564889-ever-sense-presence-deceased-loved-one-4.html. Accessed January 2, 2020.

Collerton, D., E. Perry, and I. McKeith. "Why People See Things That Are Not There: A Novel Perception and Attention Deficit Model for Recurrent Complex Visual Hallucination." *Behavioral and Brain Science* 28 (2005): 737–794.

Cottam, S., S. N. Paul, O. J. Doughty, L. Carpenter, A. Al-Mousawi, S. Karvounis, and D. J. Done. "Does Religious Belief Enable Positive Interpretation of Auditory Hallucinations? A Comparison of Religious Voice-Hearers With and Without Psychosis." *Cognitive Neuropsychiatry* 16, no. 5 (2011): 403–421.

Counts, D. A. "Near-Death and Out of Body Experiences in a Melanesian Society." *Anabiosis* 3 (1983): 115–135.

Craig, I. "Fear, Death and Sociology." *Mortality* 8, no. 3 (2003): 285–295.

Crualaoich, G. O. "The Merry Wake." In *Irish Popular Culture 1650–1850*, ed. J. S. Donnelly and K. A. Miller, 173–200. Dublin: Irish Academic Press, 1998.

Dehghan, Saeed Kamali. "Iranian Killer's Execution Halted at Last Minute by Victim's Parents." *The Guardian*, April 16, 2014. http://www.theguardian.com/world/2014/apr/16/iran-parents-halt-killer-execution.

Delespaul, P., M. deVries, and J. van Os. "Determinants of Occurrence and Recovery from Hallucinations in Daily Life." *Psychiatry and Psychiatric Epidemiology* 37 (2002): 97–104.

Dickens, C. *A Christmas Carol.* London: Chapman & Hall, 1843.

Bibliography

Diederich, N. J., C. G. Goetz, and G. T. Stebbins. "Repeated Visual Hallucinations in Parkinson's Disease as Disturbed External/Internal Perceptions: Focused Review and a New Integrated Model." *Movement Disorders* 20, no. 2 (2005): 130–140.

Donnelly, S., and J. Battley. "Relative's Experience of the Moment of Death in a Tertiary Referral Hospital." *Mortality* 15, no. 1 (2010): 81–100.

Donnelly, S. M., and C. N. Donnelly. "The Experience of the Moment of Death in a Specialist Palliative Care Unit." *Irish Medical Journal* 102, no. 5 (2009): 143–149.

Donnelly, S. M., N. Michael, and C. Donnelly. "Experience of the Moment of Death at Home." *Mortality* 11, no. 4 (2005): 352–367.

Durkheim, E. *The Elementary Forms of the Religious Life*. New York: Free Press, 1965.

Edmeads, A. "Watch with Me: A Chaplain's Perspective." *International Journal of Palliative Nursing* 13, no. 11 (2007): 549–553.

Elder, B. *And When I Die, Will I Be Dead?* Sydney: ABC Books, 1987.

Elliott, B., E. Joyce, and S. Shorvon. "Delusions, Illusions and Hallucinations in Epilepsy: Elementary Phenomena." *Epilepsy Research* 85 (2009): 162–171.

Ethier, A. M. "Death-Related Sensory Experiences." *Journal of Pediatric Oncology Nursing* 22, no. 2 (2005): 104–111.

Faccio, E., D. Romaioli, J. Dagani, and S. Cipolletta. "Auditory Hallucinations as a Personal Experience: Analysis of Non-psychiatric Voice Hearers' Narration." *Journal of Psychiatric and Mental Health Nursing* 20 (2013): 761–767.

Felek, O., and A. Knysh, eds. *Dreams and Visions in Islamic Societies*. Albany: State University of New York Press, 2012.

Fenwick, P., and S. Brayne. "End of Life Experiences: Reaching Out for Compassion, Communication and Connection-Meaning of Deathbed Visions and Coincidences." *American Journal of Hospice and Palliative Care* 28, no. 1 (2011): 7–15.

Fenwick, P., H. Lovelace, and S. Brayne. "Comfort for the Dying: Five Year Retrospective and One Year Prospective Studies of End of Life Experiences." *Archives of Gerontology and Geriatrics* 51, no. 2 (2010): 173–179.

———. "End of Life Experiences and Their Implications for Palliative Care." *International Journal of Environment Studies* 64, no. 3 (2007): 315–323.

Finucane, R. C. *Ghosts*. New York: Prometheus Books, 1996.

Firth, R. "Verbal and Bodily Greetings and Partings." In *The Interpretation of Ritual: Essays in Honour of A. I. Richards*, ed. J. S. La Fontaine, 1–38. London: Routledge, 1972.

Bibliography

Fountain, A. "Visual Hallucinations: A Prevalence Study Among Hospice Inpatients." *Palliative Medicine* 15 (2001): 19–25.

Fountain, A., and A. Kellehear. "On Prevalence Disparities in Recent Empirical Studies of Deathbed Visions." *Journal of Palliative Care* 28, no. 2 (2012): 113–115.

Fox, M. *Religion, Spirituality, and the Near-Death Experience.* London: Routledge, 2003.

Frankl, V. *Man's Search for Meaning.* London: Hodder & Stoughton, 1964.

Frazer, J. *The Belief in Immortality and the Worship of the Dead.* 3 vols. London: Macmillan, 1911–1924.

Freeman, D., and P. A. Garety. "Connecting Neurosis and Psychosis: The Direct Influence of Emotion on Delusions and Hallucinations." *Behavioral Research and Therapy* 41 (2003): 923–947.

Freeman, L., M. Caserta, D. Lund, S. Rossa, A. Dowdy, and A. Partenheimer. "Music Thanatology: Prescriptive Harp Music as Palliative Care for the Dying Patient." *American Journal of Hospice and Palliative Care* 23, no. 2 (2006): 100–104.

Freud, S. *The Future of an Illusion.* London: Hogarth Press, 1927.

———. *Reflections on War and Death.* New York: Moffat, Yard & Co., 1918.

Fridh, I., I. Bergbom, and H. Haljamae. "No Going Back: Narratives by Close Relatives of the Brain Dead Patient." *Intensive and Critical Care Nursing* 17 (2001): 263–278.

Fridh, I., A. Forsberg, and I. Bergbom. "Close Relatives' Experiences of Caring and of Physical Environment When a Loved One Dies in an ICU." *Intensive and Critical Care Nursing* 25 (2009): 111–119.

Friedenberg, J. *Visual Attention and Consciousness.* New York: Psychology Press, 2013.

Gearing, R. E., D. Alonso, A. Smolak, K. McHugh, S. Harmon, and S. Baldwin. "Association of Religion with Delusions and Hallucinations in the Context of Schizophrenia: Implications for Engagement and Adherence." *Schizophrenia Research* 126 (2011): 150–163.

Gibson, G., P. G. Mottram, D. J. Burn, J. V. Hindle, S. Landua, M. Samuel, C. S. Hurt, R. G. Brown, and K. C. M. Wilson. "Frequency, Prevalence, Incidence, and Risk Factors Associated with Visual Hallucinations in a Sample of Patients with Parkinson's Disease: A Longitudinal 4-Year Study." *Geriatric Psychiatry* 28 (2013): 626–631.

Gibson, G. C. *Wake Rites.* Gainesville: University Press of Florida, 2005.

Goldstein, E. B. *Cognitive Psychology.* Belmont, CA: Thomson Wadsworth, 2008.

Goody, E. "'Greeting,' 'Begging,' and the Presentation of Respect." In *The Interpretation of Ritual: Essays in Honour of A. I. Richards*, ed. J. S. La Fontaine, 39–71. London: Routledge, 1972.

Grainger, R. *The Unburied*. Worthing UK: Churchman Publishing, 1988.

Green, J. T. "Near-Death Experiences in Chommorro Culture." *Vital Signs* 4 (1984): 1–2, 6–7.

Grey, M. *Return from Death: An Exploration of the Near-Death Experience*. London: Arkana, 1985.

Greyson, B., and M. B. Leister. "Auditory Hallucinations Following Near-Death Experiences." *Journal of Humanistic Psychology* 44, no. 3 (2004): 320–336.

Guggenheim, B., and J. Guggenheim. *Hello from Heaven*. New York: Bantam, 1996.

Hicks, J. *Death and Eternal Life*. London: Collins, 1976.

Hill, K., and D. E. J. Linden "Hallucinatory Experiences in Non-clinical Populations." In *The Neuroscience of Hallucinations*, ed. R. Jardini, A. Cachia, P. Thomas, and D. Pins, 21–41. New York: Springer, 2013.

Holden, J., B. Greyson, and D. James. *The Handbook of Near-Death Experiences: 30 Years of Investigation*. Santa Barbara, CA: Praeger, 2009.

Hunt, R. R., and H. C. Ellis. *Fundamentals of Cognitive Psychology*. 7th ed. New York: McGraw-Hill, 2004.

International Association for Near Death Studies. "It Marked the Trajectory of My Life." January 5, 2017. https://iands.org/research/nde-research/nde-archives31/newest-accounts/1184-it-marked-the-trajectory-of-my-life.html.

James, W. *The Varieties of Religious Experience*. London: Fontana, 1960.

Johanson, D. C., and B. Edgar. *From Lucy to Language*. New York: Simon and Schuster, 1996.

Johns, L. C. "Hallucinations in the General Population." *Current Psychiatric Reports* 7 (2005): 162–167.

Kasper, B. S., E. M. Kasper, E. Pauli, and H. Stefan. "Phenomenology of Hallucinations, Illusions and Delusions as Part of Seizure Semiology." *Epilepsy and Behavior* 18 (2010): 13–23.

Kastanakis, M., and B. G. Voyer. "The Effect of Culture on Perception and Cognition: A Conceptual Framework." *Journal of Business Research* 67, no. 4 (2014): 425–433.

Kasten, E., and J. S. Geier. "Near-Death Experiences: Between Spiritual Transmigration and Psychopathological Hallucinations." *Journal of Studies in Social Sciences* 9, no. 1 (2014): 34–82.

Kellehear, A. *Dying of Cancer: The Final Year of Life*. Chur, Switzerland: Harwood Academic Publishers, 1990.

———. *Eternity and Me: The Everlasting Things in Life and Death.* Melbourne: Hill of Content, 2000.
———. *Experiences Near Death: Beyond Medicine and Religion.* New York: Oxford University Press, 1996.
———. *The Inner Life of the Dying Person.* New York: Columbia University Press, 2014.
———. "The Near-Death Experience as Status Passage." *Social Science & Medicine* 31, no. 8 (1990): 933–939.
———. "Unusual Perceptions at the End of Life: Limitations to the Diagnosis of Hallucinations in Palliative Medicine." *BMJ Supportive and Palliative Care* 7, no. 3 (2017): 238–246.
———. "Vigils for the Dying: Origin and Functions of a Persistent Tradition." *Illness, Crisis & Loss* 21, no. 2 (2013): 109–124.
Kellehear, A., V. Pogonet, R. Mindruta-Stratan, and V. Gorelco. *Care of the Dying in the Republic of Moldova.* Chisinau, Moldova: UNESCO, 2011.
———. "Deathbed Visions from the Republic of Moldova: A Content Analysis of Family Observations." *Omega: Journal of Death & Dying* 64, no. 4 (2012): 303–317.
Kimball, S. T. Introduction to *The Rites of Passage*, by A. Van Gennep, v–xix. London: Routledge & Kegan Paul, 1960.
Knapp, M. L., R. P. Hart, G. W. Friedrich, and G. M. Shulman. "The Rhetoric of Good-Bye: Verbal and Non-verbal Correlates of Leave Taking." *Speech Monographs* 40 (1973): 182–198.
Kübler-Ross, E. *On Death and Dying.* New York: Macmillan, 1969.
Kumar, S., S. Soren, and S. Chaudhury. "Hallucinations: Etiology and Clinical Implications." *Industrial Psychiatry Journal* 18, no. 2 (2009): 119–126.
Langer, A. I., G. Stanghellini, A. J. Cangas, P. H. Lysaker, L. Nieto-Munoz, J. A. Moriana, M. L. Barrigon, and A. Ambrosini. "Interpretation, Emotional Reactions, and Daily Life Implications of Hallucination-Like Experiences in Clinical and Nonclinical Populations." *Psicothema* 27, no. 1 (2015): 19–25.
Laroi, F., T. M. Luhmann, V. Bell, W. A. Christian, S. Deshpande, C. Fernyhough, J. Jenkins, and A. Woods. "Culture and Hallucinations: Overview and Future Directions." *Schizophrenia Bulletin* 40, no. 4 (2014): S213–S220.
Laroi, F., P. Marczewski, and M. Van der Linden. "Further Evidence of the Multidimensionality of Hallucinatory Predisposition: Factor Structure of a Modified Version of the Launay-Slade Hallucinations Scale in a Normal Population." *European Psychiatry* 19 (2004): 15–20.
Leslie, E. *Desperate Journeys, Abandoned Souls: True Stories of Castaways and Other Survivors.* London: Macmillan, 1988.

Bibliography

Leuba, J. H. *The Psychology of Religious Mysticism.* London: Routledge, 1925.

Li, D., O. S. Mabrouk, T. Lui, F. Tian, G. Xu, S. Rengifo, S. J. Choi, A. Mathur, C. P. Crooks, R. T. Kennedy, et al. "Asphyxia-Activated Cortico-Cardiac Signaling Accelerates Onset of Cardiac Arrest." *Proceedings of the National Academy of Science* 112, no. 16 (2015): E2073–E2082.

Linn, S. F., D. Linn, and M. Linn. *The Gifts of the Near-Death Experience.* Newburyport, MA: Hampton Roads, 2016.

Linscott, R. J., and J. van Os. "An Updated and Conservative Systematic Review and Meta-analysis of Epidemiological Evidence on Psychotic Experiences in Children and Adults: On the Pathway from Proneness to Persistence to Dimensional Expression Across Mental Disorders." *Psychological Medicine* 43 (2013): 1133–1149.

List25 Team. "25 Insane Optical Illusions That Will Leave You Dazed and Confused." List25, https://list25.com/25-incredible-optical-illusions/. Accessed January 2, 2020.

Lysaght, P. "Hospitality at Wakes and Funerals in Ireland from the Seventeenth to the Nineteenth Century: Some Evidence from the Written Record." *Folklore* 114 (2003): 403–426.

———. "Visible Death: Attitudes to the Dying in Ireland." *Marvels and Tales* 9, no. 1 (1995): 27–100.

Malinowski, B. *Magic, Science and Religion.* New York: Free Press, 1948.

Mauss, M. *The Gift: Forms and Functions in Archaic Societies.* Glencoe, IL: Free Press, 1954.

McCarthy-Jones, S., T. Trauer, A. MacKinnon, E. Sims, N. Thomas, and D. L. Copolov. "A New Phenomenological Survey of Auditory Hallucinations: Evidence for Subtypes and Implications for Theory and Practice." *Schizophrenia Bulletin* 40, no. 1 (2014): 225–235.

McCreery, C. "Perception and Hallucination: The Case for Continuity." Oxford Forum, Philosophical Paper No. 2006-1, 2006.

Miller, J. *Convinced That God Has Called Us: Dreams, Visions and the Perception of God's Will in Luke-Acts.* Leiden: Brill, 2007.

Mobbs, D., and C. Watt. "There Is Nothing Paranormal About Near-Death Experiences: How Neuroscience Can Explain Seeing Bright Lights, Meeting the Dead, or Being Convinced You Are One of Them." *Trends in Cognitive Sciences* 15, no. 10 (2011): 447–449.

Moody, R. *Life After Life.* New York: Bantam Books, 1970.

Moody, R., and P. Perry. *The Light Beyond.* New York: Bantam Books, 1988.

Morgan, B. *On Becoming God: Late Medieval Mysticism and the Modern Western Self.* New York: Fordham University Press, 2013.

Morrison, A. P. "The Interpretations of Intrusions in Psychosis: An Integrative Cognitive Approach to Hallucinations and Delusions." *Behavioral and Cognitive Psychotherapy* 29 (2001): 257–276.

Morse, M., with P. Perry. *Closer to the Light: Learning from the Near-Death Experiences of Children*. New York: Villard, 1990.

Muthumana, S. P., M. Kumari, A. Kellehear, S. Kumar, and F. Moosa. "Deathbed Visions from India: A Study of Family Observations in Northern Kerala." *Omega: Journal of Death & Dying* 62, no. 2 (2010–2011): 97–109.

Ohayon, M. M., and A. F. Schatzberg. "Prevalence of Depressive Episodes with Psychotic Features in the General Population." *American Journal of Psychiatry* 159, no. 11 (2002): 1855–1861.

Online Etymology Dictionary. s.v. "Gift *(n.)*." https://www.etymonline.com/word/gift. Accessed January 2, 2020.

Osis, K. *Deathbed Observations by Physicians and Nurses*. New York: Parapsychology Foundation, 1961.

Osis, K., and E. Haraldsson. *At the Hour of Death*. New York: Avon, 1977.

Oxford English Dictionary. s.v. "Gift *(n.)*." https://en.oxforddictionaries.com/definition/gift. Accessed January 2, 2020.

Page, S., and C. Komaromy. "Professional Performance: The Case of Unexpected and Expected Deaths." *Mortality* 10, no. 4 (2005): 294–307.

Pelling, C. "Characterizing Hallucinations Epistemically." *Synthese* 178 (2011): 437–459.

Pierre, J. M. "Hallucinations in Nonpsychotic Disorders: Toward Differential Diagnosis of 'Hearing Voices.'" *Harvard Review of Psychiatry* 18, no. 1 (2010): 22–35.

Posner, J. "Death as a Courtesy Stigma." *Essence* 1, no. 1 (1976): 39–50.

Putsch, R. W. "Ghost Illness: A Cross-Cultural Experience with the Expression of a Non-Western Tradition in Clinical Practice." *American Indian and Alaska Mental Health Research* 2, no. 2 (1988): 6–26.

Read, T., and J. Wuest. "Daughters Caring for Dying Parents: A Process of Relinquishing." *Qualitative Health Research* 17, no. 7 (2007): 932–944.

Regnard, C. L., and S. Tempest. *Managing Opioid Adverse Effects: A Guide to Symptom Relief in Advanced Disease*. 4th ed. Hale, UK: Hochland and Hochland.

Rich, K. R. *The Red Devil: To Hell with Cancer—and Back*. New York: Crown, 1999.

Ring, K. "Amazing Grace: The Near-Death Experience as Compensatory Gift." *Journal of Near-Death Studies* 10, no. 1 (1991): 11–39.

———. *Life at Death: A Scientific Investigation of the Near-Death Experience*. New York: Coward, McCann & Geoghegan, 1980.

Sacks, O. *Hallucinations*. London: Picador, 2013.
Saint-Exupéry, A. de. *The Little Prince*. New York: Reynal & Hitchcock, 1943.
"[Serious] Redditors Who Have Been Clinically Dead and Then Revived/Resuscitated: What Did Dying Feel Like? Did You See Anything Whilst Passed On?" Reddit, https://www.reddit.com/r/AskReddit/comments/332k1c/serious_redditors_who_have_been_clinically_dead/cqh8t7e. Accessed January 2, 2020.
Seymour, J. E. "Revisiting Medicalization and 'Natural' Death." *Social Science & Medicine* 49, no. 5 (1999): 691–704.
Shushan, G. *Conceptions of the Afterlife in Early Civilizations*. London: Continuum, 2009.
Siegal, R. K. "The Psychology of Life After Death." *American Psychologist* 35, no. 10 (1980): 911–931.
Simmel, G. "Note on Faithfulness and Gratitude." In *The Sociology of Georg Simmel*, ed. K. H. Wolff, 379–395. New York: Free Press, 1950.
Steel, C., G. Haddock, N. Tarrier, A. Picken, and C. Barrowclough. "Auditory Hallucinations and Post-traumatic Stress Disorder with Schizophrenia and Substance Abuse Disorder." *Journal of Nervous and Mental Disease* 199, no. 9 (2011): 709–711.
Temmingh, H., D. J. Stein, S. Seedat, and D. R. Williams. "The Prevalence and Correlates of Hallucinations in a General Population Sample: Findings from the South African Stress and Health Study." *African Journal of Psychiatry* 14 (2011): 211–217.
Thoreau, H. D. *Walden*. 1854. Repr., New York: Houghton Mifflin, 1906.
Tolstoy, L. *The Death of Ivan Illyich*. 1883. Repr., New York: Bantam, 1981.
Tracy, D. K., and S. S. Shergill. "Mechanisms Underlying Auditory Hallucinations—Understanding Perception Without Stimulus." *Brain Sciences* 3 (2013): 642–669.
Turner, V. *The Ritual Process: Structure and Anti-structure*. New York: Aldine de Gruyter, 1969.
Van Gennep, A. *The Rites of Passage*. 1908. Repr., London: Routledge & Kegan Paul, 1960.
Van Lommel, P. "About the Continuity of Consciousness." *Advances in Experimental Medicine and Biology* 550 (2004): 115–132.
Van Os, J., R. J. Linscott, I. Myin-Germeys, P. Delespaul, and L. Krabbendam. "A Systematic Review and Meta-analysis of the Psychotic Continuum: Evidence for a Psychosis-Prone-Persistence-Impairment Model of Psychotic Disorder." *Psychological Medicine* 39 (2009): 179–195.
Varese, F., E. Barkus, and R. P. Bentall. "Dissociation Mediates the Relationship Between Childhood Trauma and Hallucination-Proneness." *Psychological Medicine* 42 (2012): 1025–1036.

Walker, J., C. Holm Hanson, P. Martin, A. Sawhney, P. Thekkumpurath, C. Beale, S. Symeonides, L. Wall, G. Murray, and M. Sharpe. "Prevalence of Depression in Adults with Cancer: A Systematic Review." *Annals of Oncology* 24, no. 4 (2012): 895–900.

Wall, P. *Pain: The Science of Suffering*. London: Weidenfield & Nicholson, 1999.

Watkins, J. *Hearing Voices: A Common Human Experience*. Melbourne: Hill of Content, 1998.

Weber, M. *The Sociology of Religion*. Boston: Beacon Press, 1965.

West, T. G. *Seeing What Others Cannot See: The Hidden Advantages of Visual Thinkers and Differently Wired Brains*. New York: Prometheus Books, 2017.

Wilson, I. *The After Death Experience*. New York: Sidgwick & Jackson, 1987.

Wilson, R. S., Y. Tang, N. T. Aggarwal, D. W. Gilley, J. J. McCann, J. L. Bienias, and D. A. Evans. "Hallucinations, Cognitive Decline, and Death in Alzheimer's Disease." *Neuroepidemiology* 26 (2006): 68–75.

Windt, J. M. "Altered Consciousness in Philosophy." In *Altering Consciousness: Multidisciplinary Perspectives*, ed. E. Cardena and M. Winkelman, 229–254. Santa Barbara, CA: Praeger, 2011.

Woodhouse, J. "A Personal Reflection on Sitting at the Bedside of a Dying Loved One." *International Journal of Palliative Nursing* 10, no. 11 (2004): 537–541.

Woods, A., N. Jones, M. Bernini, F. Callard, B. Alderson-Day, J. C. Badcock, V. Bell, C. C. H. Cook, T. Csordas, C. Humpston, et al. "Interdisciplinary Approaches to the Phenomenology of Auditory Verbal Hallucinations." *Schizophrenia Bulletin* 40, no. 4 (2014): S246–S254.

Wouters, C. "The Quest for New Rituals in Dying and Mourning: Changes in the We–I Balance." *Body and Society* 8, no. 1 (2002): 1–27.

Wright, K. "Relationships with Death: The Terminally Ill Talk About Dying." *Journal of Marital and Family Therapy* 29, no. 4 (2003): 439–454.

Zaleski, C. *Otherworld Journeys: Accounts of Near-Death Experience in Medieval and Modern Times*. New York: Oxford University Press, 1987.

Index

academic explanation, of NDEs, 10, 32–33, 109–110
adult dead, 172n2
advice and direction: from afterlife contact, 80, 83, 87–95; during DBVs, 85; during NDEs, 84–85; as supportive, 84–86; during VBs, 81–82, 85
after-death communication, 167n37. *See also* visions, of bereaved (VBs)
aftereffects, of NDEs, 19
afterlife, the: appearance of, 89–91; belief in, 5–6, 94; mythology on, 86; NDEs describing, 87, 90–91; religion and, 6, 84, 91, 157; secular society and, 91; stories of, 87
afterlife contact: absence of, 150, 153, 156; adult dead and, 172n2; advice and direction from, 80–95; animal and child visitors and, 172n2; anthropologic perspectives on, xi, 6, 86–87; behavior patterns of, xiii; as beings of light, xi, 70–74, 76; context of, 107–110, 155–156; cultural perspectives on, xi, 19, 20; dreams of, 82; duration of, 69–70, 87–89; by familiars, 75–76; farewell behavior and, 76–79; fear of, 83–84, 92–93; frequency of, 16, 53, 55, 120, 150; gifts from, 116–130; greetings from, 63–69, 108; as hallucination, 5, 6, 20, 21–38, 91; information received from, 86–87; inspiration from, 119; interpersonal experience and, 151; Islamic societies and, 82; Japan and, 152–153; as life changing, xiii, 99–103; messages from, 67–69, 80–95, 116–117, 176–177n3; NDEs and, 17, 18, 70–74, 84–85; out-of-body

193

Index

afterlife contact (*cont.*)
experiences and, 21; patterns of, 17, 64–65; perceptions and, 32, 54–55; personal growth and support from, 85–86; as positive, xii, 17–18, 64, 99, 102–103, 157; reasons for, x–xi, xii, 83, 86–92, 156; religion and, 6, 19, 70, 82, 84; as rite of passage, 107; social/cultural experience of, xi–xii, 7, 9–10, 83; stigma around, 106–107, 117–118; as unpleasant, 123–124. *See also* deathbed visions (DBVs); visions, of bereaved (VBs)
afterlife visitors, 75–76; absence of, 150, 153, 156; emergency social services as, 144; familiars as, 84–85
Alexander, Eben, 86–87
alone, feeling, 135
Alzheimer's disease, 25, 28, 34
Angela (deceased visitor), 119–120, 127
animal and child visitors, 172n2
Anita (visited person), 4, 53
anthropologic perspectives: on afterlife contact, xi, 6, 86–87; on hallucinations, 23; on transitional hominids, 13–14; of Trobriand Islands culture, 88–89
apophenia, 48–49
apparitions. *See* afterlife contact
appearance, of the afterlife, 89–91
Aston, Guy, 66
atheism, and NDEs, 56
attachment: the dead and, 92–93; loss and, 91–92
auditory hallucinations, 36
Auschwitz, 51

Balal (murderer), 82
Barrett, William, 3–4
Barry (visited person), 108, 112
Beal, Christine, 66
Becker, Carl, 153
behavior patterns, of afterlife contact, xiii
beings of light: afterlife contact and, xi, 70–74, 76; characteristics of, 13–14; children seeing, 12; continuance customs and, 73–74, 76; DBVs and, 99–100, 143–144; as Emergency Social Services, 75–76; farewell behavior of, 76–79; genders of, 164n16; gifts from, 122–123; Jesus as, 173n2; as life changing, 99–100; as memorable and positive, 17–18, 73–74; NDEs and, 17, 18, 70–74, 144, 164n16; peace and well-being from, 11, 13, 71–72; review of life by, 81; Saul of Tarsus and, 80–81; supreme being as, 12, 70–71; types of, 70–72; uniform of, 73–74
belief, in an afterlife, 5–6; denial and, 94
Belief in Immortality and the Worship of the Dead, The (Frazer), 83
bereavement, 58–59, 92–93; hospice and palliative care and, 27; NDEs and, 86
bereavement communication, 119
bereavement visions. *See* visions, of bereaved (VBs)
biases, and perception, 40–42, 45–46
Bible, visits from the dead in, 19
binary thinking, 43
biographical context, VBs and, 81, 107–109
Blanes, Ruy, xii–xiii

Index

Book of Acts, 80–81
"bottom-up" and "top-down" processes, 47–48
brain, and consciousness, 6–7
brain stimulation, hallucinations and, 31

cemetery visits, 137
cerebral anoxia, and NDEs, 32
ceremonies, as rites of passage, 103–104
characteristics, of beings of light, 13–14
children, seeing beings of light, 12
color blindness studies, 43
consciousness, and the brain, 6–7
context: of afterlife contact, 107–110, 155–156; as biographical, 81, 107–109
continuance: beings of light and, 73–74, 76; greetings of afterlife contact as, 67–76
control, over dying experience, 141–142
convergent evolution, 49–50
"courtesy stigma," 118
cultural perspectives: on afterlife contact, xi, 19, 20; of dying experience, 33; fear, of afterlife contact and, 83–84; on hallucinations, 33–38; on idiosyncratic perceptions, 35; on NDEs, 32; on perception, 41, 47
customs, regarding the dead: greetings and, 67, 69, 70, 74–75, 82; loss of, 86

Damascus, Syria, 80–81
DBVs. *See* deathbed visions (DBVs)

dead, the: as adults, 172n2; attachment and, 92–93; Bible and, 19; customs regarding, 86; DBVs and NDEs joining, 128–129; fear and, 91–93; gifts from, 118–130; greetings and, 67, 69, 70, 74–75, 82; heaven and, 79; mutilation of, 84, 93–94; as people, 127–128; recently dead contrasted with long dead, 14; repaying, 126–128; rites for, 83–84; vigils from, 143–149. *See also* afterlife contact
death: facing, 100; grief and, 7, 141; life expectancy and, 111; neuroscience researching, 5, 6; perceptions of, 50–56; personality after, 94; rites of passage and, 105–106; rituals and, 92–93; spirituality and, 100; survival over, x, 5, 6, 94, 95; vigils and, 138–149
"Death and the Reintegration of the Group" (Malinowski), 92
deathbed studies, ix–x, 4
deathbed vigils, 137–142
deathbed visions (DBVs), 5–6, 18–19, 58; advice from, 85; beings of light and, 99–100, 143–144; biographical context of, 107–109; farewell behavior and, 78; frequency of, 53; gifts from, 120–121, 127–129; "go back and live" instruction, 84, 85, 88, 129; as hallucinations, 26; joining the dead and, 128–129; as life changing, 99–100; of the long dead, 16–17; of the recently dead, 14–16; as vigils, 143–144, 146–147, 154–155

Index

deathwatch, 138, 139, 140. *See also* vigils
deceased visitors: Angela, 119–120, 127; animal and child, 172n2; familiars, 75–76, 84–85; Heather, 115–118, 126, 176–177n3; Hmong father, 123–124; Nan, 63–65, 66, 81; Salish father, 123–124; Scott, 85; Valerie, x, 67–69
Dehghan, Saeed Kamali, 82
delirium, near death, 5, 25
dementia, 17, 25
depression, and hallucinations, 25
diagnosis, of hallucinations, 28, 35–36
discomfort or distress, afterlife contact causing, xii
disordered thinking, near death, 5
dissociative experiences, 27, 28
Donnelly, Sinead and C. N., 138–139
dopamine system: of human body, 30; NDEs and, 33
dreams, of afterlife contact, 82
duration, of afterlife contact, 69–70, 87–89
dying and bereaved, the, "threshold people," 140
dying experience, 33; control over, 141–142
dyslexia, 49

Elder, Bruce, 11
emergency social services (afterlife visitors), 75–76, 144
emotions, NDEs and, 33
encounters, after death, 91, 174n11; eschatology, 6, 89; pareschatology, 86

epilepsy, 27–28
eschatology (last encounters after death), 6, 89, 91, 174n11
Espírito Santo, Diana, xii–xiii
evolution, convergent, 49–50
exchange relationship, and gifts, 125–130
expressions, of grief, 92–93

facing death, 100
false-positive perceptions, 48
familiars (afterlife visitors), 75–76, 84–85
farewell behavior: of beings of light, 76–79; DBVs and, 78; of the dying, 77–78; vigils as, 143
fear: of afterlife contact, 83–84, 92–93; of sharing afterlife contact experience, 106–107
feeling alone, 135
Fenwick, Peter, 99–100
Finucane, R. C., 84, 90
first encounter after death (pareschatology), 86, 91, 174n11
flying, out-of-body experiences, 11
folkloric perspectives, on afterlife contact, xi
Fountain, Averil, 25
Frankl, Victor, 51
Frazer, James, 83, 84, 89–90
freedom, of life course, 110–111
frequency: of afterlife contact, 16, 53, 55, 120, 150; of DBVs, 53; of farewell behavior, 77; of hallucinations, 24–25; of idiosyncratic perceptions, 23–24, 25, 26–27; of VBs, 152–153
Freud, Sigmund, 52
front-door rituals study, 66
funerals, 105, 137, 141

gender and sexual identity, 105, 164n16
genetics, and perception, 43
Gershwin, Ira and George, 137
ghost sightings. *See* afterlife contact
Gift, The (Mauss), 180n3
gifts: from beings of light, 122–123; exchange relationship and, 125–130; messages as, 116–117; NDE guidance and, 122–124; as reassurance, 126–127; reciprocity and, 124–130; from VBs and NDEs, 117, 118–120
"go back and live," instruction from DBVs, 84
Goldstein, Bruce, 47
goodbyes. *See* farewell behavior
Goody, Esther, 65–66
greetings, of afterlife contact, 63, 64; absence of, 71–74; beings of light and, 70–74, 76; continuance customs and, 67–76; of familiars and emergency social services, 75–76; formal, 69; as social/cultural, 65–67, 74–75; study on front-door, 66; taxonomy of, 74–75; as verbal, 67–69
Grey, Margot, 100–101
grief: death and, 7, 141; expressions of, 92–93; loss and attachment and, 91–92; perceptions of, 50–56; preparing for, 77–78; rituals of, 84, 93–94
growth and support, from afterlife contact, 85–86
Guardian, The (newspaper), 81–82
Guggenheim, Bill and Judy, x, 79, 102–103

hallucinations, 29; afterlife contact as, 5, 6, 20, 91; Alzheimer's disease and dementia and, 25; anthropologic perspectives on, 23; as auditory, 36; brain stimulation and, 32; depression and, 25; diagnosis of, 28, 35–36; as distressing, 25–26; at end of life, 24–25; frequency of, 24–25; as idiosyncratic perceptions, 23–26, 34–35; mental health and, 30; as NDEs, 21–22; pharmacology and, 28, 30, 33; physiology and, 30–31; psychiatry explaining, 21–22; psychotic experience as, 24; social/cultural experience and, 33–38; studies on, 31; triggers of, 30; VBs as, 27
hearing voices, 36
Heather (deceased visitor), 115–118, 126, 145, 176–177n3
heaven, and the dead, 79
Helen (cancer patient), 50–51
Hello from Heaven (Guggenheim and Guggenheim), 79, 102–103
Hervey Islanders, 85
Hmong father (deceased visitor), 123–124
hospice and palliative care, xi–xii, 4, 25, 27; bereavement and, 27; deathbed vigils and, 138–139; idiosyncratic perceptions and, 35
"How Neuroscience Can Explain Seeing Bright Lights, Meeting the Dead, or Being Convinced You Are One of Them" (2011), 32
hypnogogic and hypnopompic perceptions, 26
hypnosis argument, 56

ideas, of reality, 43–44
idiosyncratic perceptions: cultural perspectives on, 35; DBVs and, 26; frequency of, 23–24, 25, 26–27; hallucinations as, 23–26, 34–35; hospice and palliative care and, 35; hypnogogic and hypnopompic, 26; NDEs and, 26; as negative, 25; psychopathology and, 25, 28, 29; self-inducing, 29–30; VBs and, 27
immortality, 89–90, 93, 94
India study (2009), ix, 4, 26–27, 120
information: from afterlife contact, 86–87; NDE gifts as, 121–122
inner voices, 35
inquiry, intellectual, 7–9
inspiration, from afterlife contact, 119
instruction, from DBVs, "go back and live," 84, 85, 88, 129
intellectual inquiry, 7–9
interpersonal experience, and afterlife contact, 151
Iran, 81–82
Islamic societies, and afterlife contact, 82

Jake (author's friend), 115–118, 150
James, William, 36
Japan, and afterlife contact, 152–153
Jesus, as being of light, 173n2
joining the dead, 128–129
judicial system, 45, 48

Kimball, Solon, 104
Kübler-Ross, Elisabeth, 114

last encounters after death (eschatology), 6, 89, 91, 174n11
"Let It Be" (song), 126–127
Leuba, James, 176n2
Life after Life (Moody), 57
life changing: afterlife contact as, xiii, 15–16, 99–103; beings of light as, 99–100; DBVs as, 99–100; life experiences as, 96–99; mystical experiences as, 101–102; NDEs as, 100–103; VBs as, 102–103, 116–118
life course, freedom of, 110–111
life expectancy, 111
life experiences, as life changing, 96–99
light phenomena during NDEs, 70–71. *See also* beings of light
Little Prince, The (Saint-Exupéry), 136
long dead, the, 16–17; recently dead contrasted with, 14
loss: attachment and, 91–92; of customs of the dead, 86

Malinowski, Bronislaw, 88–89, 92–93, 94
Mauss, Marcel, 125, 180n3
McCartney, Paul, 119, 126–127
medical emergency, and NDEs, 10–11
memorable and positive: afterlife contact as, xii, 17–18, 64; NDEs as, 100–102
mental health: hallucinations and, 30; idiosyncratic perceptions and, 35
mental stability, questioning, 19
messages, from afterlife contact, 67–69, 80–95, 176n3; as gifts, 116–117

Index

modern world, mystical experience and, 148
Moldova study, ix–x, 16–17, 26–27, 120–121
Moody, Raymond, 12, 57, 70
Morgan, Ben, 135
Morse, Melvin, 12, 70–71
mortuary processes, 93
mutilation, of the dead, 84, 93–94
mystical experiences, x, 36, 48; as life changing, 101–102; modern world and, 148; as religious, 176n2; stigma around, 117–118; vigils as, 142
mythology, afterlife, 86

naive realism, 29, 37
Nan (deceased visitor), 63–65, 66, 81
near-death experiences (NDEs): academics explaining, 10, 32–33, 109–110; aftereffects of, 19; the afterlife and, 87, 90–91; afterlife contact and, 17, 18, 70–74, 84–85; atheism and, 56; beings of light and, 17, 18, 70–74, 144, 164n16; bereavement and, 86; biographical context of, 107–110; cerebral anoxia and, 32; of children, 12; cultural perspectives on, 32; descriptions of the afterlife and, 90–91; dopamine system and, 33; emotions surrounding, 33; gifts and, 117, 118–124; as hallucinations, 21–22, 33; idiosyncratic perceptions and, 26; joining the dead and, 128–129; as life changing, 100–103; light phenomena during, 70–71; medical emergencies and, 10–11; as memorable and positive, 100–102; out-of-body experience during, 11; perceptions of, 53–55; during resuscitation, 10, 71, 73, 88; skepticism and, 87; spirituality and, 122, 129; transitional hominids and, 13–14; vigils and, 144–145, 146–148
neuroimaging studies, 31
neuroscience research, of dying, 5, 6, 17
New Age movement, 6, 17, 106

offerings, to the dead, 83–84
On Death and Dying (Kübler-Ross), 114
opioid system: of human body, 28; NDEs and, 33
optical illusions, 44
Otherworld Journeys (Zaleski), 101
out-of-body experiences, 5, 10, 57–58, 144; academics explaining, 10, 32–33, 109–110; afterlife contact during, 21; as dissociative experiences, 27, 28; flying during, 11
Oxford English Dictionary, 124, 125

Pacific, the, 83, 89–90, 106
palliative care. *See* hospice and palliative care
pareschatology (first encounter after death), 91, 174n11; and religion, 86
Parkinson's disease, 24, 28, 32, 34
pathology, and idiosyncratic perceptions, 35
patient-family-doctor relationship, 35
patterns, of afterlife contact, 17, 64–65

Index

Paul (apostle), 80–81
peace and well-being, 63–65, 85; being of light bringing, 11, 13, 71–72
people, the dead as, 127–128
perception: afterlife contact and, 32, 54–55; apophenia and, 48–49; biases and, 40–42, 45–46; cultural perspectives on, 41, 47; of dying and grieving, 50–56; dyslexia and, 49; false-positive, 48; genetics and, 43; near death, 53–54; perspective and, 54–56; physical environment and, 46–47; psychology of, 45–48, 152; as selective, 45; societal ideas of, 41
Perry, Paul, 70
personality, after death, 94
perspectives: anthropologic, xi, 6, 13–14, 23, 86–87, 88–89; cultural, xi, 19, 20, 32, 33–38, 41, 47, 83–84; perception influenced by, 54–56
pharmacology and pharmacotherapy, 28, 30, 33
physical environment, and perception, 46–47
physiology, and hallucinations, 30–31
piano teacher (visited person), 14–16, 145–146
polypharmacy, and hallucinations, 25
pop psychology, 106
positive experience, of afterlife contact, xii, 17–18, 64, 99, 102–103, 157
Posner, Judith, 118
preparing for grief, 77–78
prevalence. *See* frequency
processes, "bottom-up" and "top-down," 47–48
Proof of Heaven (Alexander), 86–87
pseudo-hallucinations. *See* idiosyncratic perceptions
psychiatry: hallucinations explained by, 21–22; religion intersecting, 37
psychology: biographical context of, 109; of perception, 45–48, 152; pop, 106
The Psychology of Religious Mysticism (Leuba), 176n2
psychopathology, and idiosyncratic perceptions, 25, 28, 29
psychotic experience as hallucination, 24
Putsch, Robert W., 123–124

rational humanism, 106
reality, ideas of, 43–44
reasons, for afterlife contact, x–xi, xii, 83, 86–92, 156
recently dead, the, visits from, 63–65; as life changing, 15–16; the long dead contrasted with, 14
reciprocity, and gifts, 124–130
religion: the afterlife and, 6, 84, 91, 157; DBVs and, 19; dreams and, 82; mystical experience and, 176n2; pareschatology and, 86; society intersecting, 37; supreme being of light and, 70
repayment, of DBV gifts, 126–128
research, on hallucinations, 34
resuscitation, NDEs during, 10, 71, 73, 88
review, of life, 81
Rich, Katherine Russell, 13, 71–72, 107, 153, 155–156
Ring, Ken, 68, 90, 101

Index

rites: for the dead, 83–84; of separation for dying, 105–106
rites of passage, 103–112; afterlife contact as, 107; ceremonies as, 103–104; lack of, 105–106
Rites of Passage, The (van Gennep), 103–104
rituals: death and, 92–93, 105–106; front-door, 66; of grief, 84, 93–94
Roy (author's deceased friend), 113–114

Saint Exupéry, Antoine de, 136
Salish father (deceased visitor), 123–124
Sally (visited person), 63–65, 66, 81, 107, 172n1
Saul of Tarsus, 80–81
schizophrenia, and hallucinations, 30
scientific perspective, on afterlife contact, 6; anthropology, xi, 86–87; neuroscience, 5, 17, 31; psychiatry, 21–22, 37; psychology, 45–48, 106, 109, 152; psychopathology, 25, 28, 29
Scott (deceased visitor), 85
secular society, 82, 92, 94, 147; afterlife and, 91; supernatural beings and, 19, 86; vigils and, 142, 148
"sent back," 129
separation for dying, rites of, 105–106
sexual and gender identity, 105, 164n16
Sharia law, 82
sightings of the dead. *See* afterlife contact
skepticism, and NDEs, 87
social/cultural experience: of afterlife contact, xi–xiii, 7, 9–10, 23, 83; biases and, 40–42; customs for the dead and, 86; of death and grief, 7, 83; farewell behavior as, 77–79; gift exchange as, 124–130; greetings as, 65–67, 74–75; grief rituals, 84; of hallucinations, 33–38; idiosyncratic perceptions and, 29–30; life course and, 110–111; quality of, 9–10; religion intersecting, 37; rites of passage as, 103–112; sexual and gender identity as, 105; story illustrating, 7–9; vigils as, 135–142
Social Life of Spirits, The (Blanes and Espírito Santo), xii–xiii
Sonia (visited person), x, 67–68
spirits of the dead, 93, 104
spirituality: death and, 100; NDEs and, 122, 129
stereograms, 44
stigmas, around afterlife contact, 106–107, 117–118
stories, of the afterlife, 87
studies: on color blindness, 43; deathbed, ix–x, 4; farewell behavior of the dying, 77–78; on front-door rituals, 66; on hallucinations, 31; on idiosyncratic perception, 23–24; in India (2009), ix, 4, 26–27, 120; in Moldova, ix–x, 16–17, 26–27, 120–121
supernatural beings, and secular society, 19
supreme being of light, 12, 71; religion and, 70
survival, after death, x, 6
survival, over death, x, 95; denial of, 94; evidence of, 5, 6

taxonomy, of greeting the dead, 74–75
Thoughts for the Times on War and Death (Freud), 52
"threshold people," the dying and bereaved, 140
transitional hominids, 13–14
Traverso, Veronique, 66
triggers, of hallucinations, 30
Trobriand Islanders, 88–89
tunnel sensations, 32
Turner, Victor, 140
Twilight Zone, The (show), 58

uniform, of beings of light, 73–74
United Kingdom, 25–26, 27
unpleasant afterlife contact, 123–124
unusual perceptions. *See* idiosyncratic perceptions

Valerie (deceased visitor), x, 67–69
van Gennep, Arnold, 103–104
VBs. *See* visions, of bereaved (VBs)
verbal greeting, from afterlife contact, 67–69, 108
Victorian Spiritualists, 91
vigils, xiii, 135–137; DBVs as, 143–144, 146–147, 154–155; by the dead, 143–149; deathbed, 137–142; as farewell behavior, 143; NDEs and, 144–145, 146–148; secular society and, 142, 148; social purposes of, 140–142
visions, of bereaved (VBs), 10, 27, 29, 50, 56, 58, 167–168n37; advice from, 81–82, 85;
biographical context and, 81, 107–109; frequency of, 152–153; gifts from, 117, 118–124; greetings during, 66–67; Heather as, 115–118; *Hello from Heaven* (book) on, 79; as life changing, 102–103, 116–118
visitations, by the dead. *See* afterlife contact; *specific topics*
visited persons: Anita, 4, 53; author, 11; Barry, 108, 112; piano teacher, 14–16, 145–146; Sally, 63–65, 66, 81, 107, 172n1; Sonia, x, 67–68
visitors, deceased: absence of, 150, 153, 156; from afterlife, 75–76; Angela, 119–120, 127; animal and child, 172n2; emergency social services as, 144; familiars as, 75–76, 84–85; Heather, 115–118, 126; Hmong father, 123–124; Nan, 63–65, 66, 81; Salish father, 123–124; Scott, 85; Valerie, x, 67–69
visits, to cemeteries, 137
vocal perceptions. *See* auditory hallucinations
voices: hearing, 36; inner, 35

wakes, 138, 140, 142
watching over. *See* vigils
West, the, 104, 105, 147–148
West, Thomas, 49
Wilson, Ian, 11
Windt, Jennifer, 36
Wysocki, Sheila (née Gibbons), 119–120, 127

Zaleski, Carol, 101

GPSR Authorized Representative: Easy Access System Europe, Mustamäe tee 50, 10621 Tallinn, Estonia, gpsr.requests@easproject.com